FROM START
TO FINISH

FROM START TO FINISH

A Corporal's View of the RAF

A. Barker

JANUS PUBLISHING COMPANY
London, England

First published in Great Britain 1997
by Janus Publishing Company
Edinburgh House, 19 Nassau Street
London W1N 7RE

British Library Cataloguing-in-Publication Data.
A catalogue record for this book is available from the British Library.

ISBN 1 85756 302 6

Cover design Nick Eagleton

Photoset by Keyboard Services, Luton
Printed and bound in England by
Antony Rowe Ltd
Chippenham, Wiltshire

Preface

The incidents in this narrative are true, although some names have been changed. I have endeavoured to show the humorous side of the RAF men and also the dangerous duties they had to undergo in wartime.

In 1937 I saw the last Hendon Air Display and took part in lining the route for George VI's Coronation. As a mechanic I then served on 66 Squadron at Duxford on Gloucester Gauntlets and then on the earliest Spitfires to be issued to the RAF.

After the outbreak of the Second World War I was posted to help start the new Squadron of 219 under 'Batchy Atcherley', the famous pilot who won the World's Speed Record in a Gloster Grebe, and later the Schneider Trophy in a Supermarine S6 at 331.6 mph. He was later to become an Air Marshal.

In January of 1940 I was posted to 16 Army Co-operation Squadron in the Expeditionary Force in France and was nearly taken prisoner. The planes were Lysanders. I was to bid farewell to the first NZ RAF man to be shot down and killed. Later I was to join 203 Overseas Squadron on Blenheims serving in Aden, the Middle East, throughout three years of the Desert Campaign and El-Alamein, and then flew over to India with the squadron and their new Wellingtons.

This book is a follow-up to *One of Thirteen* published in 1992.

I wish to thank Richard M. Challoner, BA, MA, for his research work of 203 Squadron.

Arthur Barker, 1997

Contents

1

War Clouds

THE year was 1936 and ominous war clouds were gathering in the skies. Alfred was about to lock up the shop in Derby city and return home to the farm. Opposite the butcher's shop in Siddals Road were two young mechanics. They were installing Dorman Long diesel engines into British-made lorries. They both nodded to Alfred and shouted, 'Come over here and look at these wonderful German engines.' At this period of time almost every local haulier was turning over to the German-designed diesel engines which were cheaper to run than our petrol-driven vehicles.

No sooner had the boys uttered the words when Mr Napper, the one-armed owner of a transport company, deftly drove his lorry to the side of the garage and exclaimed, 'Here's another one for you to change the engine on, lads.' Then he quickly transferred to another of his newly converted lorries and with a swift movement of his arm he steered the vehicle on to the road. One of the mechanics turned to Alfred and said, 'What about Hitler then? I don't believe all the papers say about those Germans only having picks and shovels for rifles. Or them trying to tell us they've got cardboard and wooden aeroplanes, not when they can build engines like these diesels.'

'Oh no,' said Alfred. 'I also hear that Rolls-Royce are doing a lot of overtime on new aero engines.'

The two young men then both turned to face Alfred and told him, 'We are thinking of going to Rolls-Royce to work as they are taking on engineers in their expansion programme.'

Alfred replied, 'Only this morning, whilst delivering orders around town I was passing the tramway depot, I saw on show there the Supermarine S6 seaplane.' This design by Michael had just won the world's air-speed record.

Little did Alfred realise that in a year or two's time he would be in the RAF as a mechanic and serving under the very pilot who had flown this plane. He was Wing Commander Richard Atcherly, who was commonly called ' Batchy Atcherly'. He would also meet up with the same two young men as Rolls-Royce engineers when they were sent to sort out the early troubles of Spitfires on 66 Squadron at Duxford in 1938.

Alfred was one of a family of thirteen children and remembered his own brothers returning home from the First World War when he was three years old. Now the threat of a second war was imminent and although he was already a special policeman he now decided to join the RAF.

Late in the December of 1936 he received a letter informing him to report to West Drayton for interview with possible entry into the RAF. It was the first time that Alfred had been away from the security of a farming family. After duly reporting and submitting his credentials to the echelons of power, he was examined by the RAF doctor. 'You're a bit thin me lad, have you had any serious illnesses?'

'Only anthrax,' replied Alfred.

'That's a serious illness. Were you in hospital?'

'Oh no,' said Alfred. 'The local doctor just laid my arm on the desk, injected me, then cut the hard core out of the swollen infected part on my wrist. He had then ground up M and B tablets, stuck the powder in the wound, and given him a couple of tablets to swallow. Alfred had then walked the one and a half miles home.

Disbelievingly, the medic took another interested look at Alfred, inspected his teeth and said, 'You've got an excellent set of teeth which shows you've a pretty good constitution, so I'll pass you as OK.'

Having passed his medical on the strength of his teeth, he was now to go and collect his dinner; the RAF always had good dinners ready for new entrants. He joined the long queue in the dining hall with the other 'sprogs'; never before had he been in a queue so swiftly dished out with dinner.

As the queue shrank, Alfred, who was in his best suit, now faced the hot counter. Plated dinners appeared like magic from its bowels. The RAF orderly, with the deftness of a publican, dispatched two plates loaded with meat, potatoes, peas and gravy, down the counter. A barman with two pints of ale could not have done better.

The man in front of Alfred managed to stop his plate in the nick of time before it could slide out of control on to the floor. Alfred had never before been served dinner in this way and caught the plate firmly in the midriff. The contents of the plate were splattered decoratively across the front of his best suit.

'Thank you very much,' said Alfred in mock appreciation.

'Don't thank me, thank the Lord you've got it,' replied the orderly.

Alfred went and sat down at a table with an Eastender who appeared to Know-it-all: 'What the f—ing hell have you done to your f—ing suit? If I was you I'd go and give that f—ing orderly a f—ing good telling off.'

Coming from a farming family of the Victorian era and with a strict upbringing, Alfred had never heard so many f—ings in his life. But later in his career he would realise that there were many more descriptive adjectives used in service life.

He was duly called into the office again. The NCO in charge looked at him with disbelief in his eyes and said, 'Do you really want to join the RAF? You're still sworn in as a special policeman.'

Alfred replied in the affirmative. 'Then I'll have to ring up the Derby Police and get you released. Who's your Chief Constable?'

'Captain Rawlings,' he replied, and was in due course signed on for a period of three years. He and the rest of the entry were eventually dispatched to Uxbridge for the square-bashing course, with a view to making this motley crew into one entity, a uniformed, saluting, serving mob. Which of the Royal family they would serve under was still a question, as the monarchy was under stress, as the Prince Edward and Mrs Simpson affair was rife.

Prince Edward, King George V and the future King George VI

When Alfred was eventually dispatched to his billet, the overall man in charge was a charismatic personality, Warrant Officer McGee. He was duly shown how to make his bed, unmake his bed and remake his bed. How to sew on buttons, crease his trousers and sew holes in his socks and, above all, how to subscribe 3d. out of his weekly pay of 12s. for the upkeep of the barrack block. Should there be breakages, a few more pennies would be extracted from his pay.

The orderliness of service life, the facility of baths and sport compensated for loss of his previously boring job of cleaning out cowsheds and farmyards and cutting up meat.

When they were eventually issued uniforms, they were First World War uniforms of full-necked tunics, knee-breeches and puttees, along with First World War rifles and bayonets. The newer open-necked tunics were just beginning to be issued. The greatest of empires on earth was still thinking in terms of the First World War and its out-dated equipment. Baldwin and other ministers were too engrossed with internal problems to worry about a jumped-up-corporal called Hitler.

One lunch time Alfred was in a long queue for dinner and was finally served with nicely cooked fresh herrings. He sat down beside Sam, a clean-looking lad, but he had a rather queer far-seeing stare in his eyes. Alfred began to enjoy his herring but suddenly noticed that Sam had picked up a herring in his two hands and was running his mouth along the length of it, like someone playing a mouth organ.

'Good God,' said Alfred, 'Don't you use knives and forks in your house?'

'Yes, but only to throw at one another. You see that tea bucket over there? Well my father invented the spout on it.'

On looking at it Alfred could only see a small protrusion to stop the tea dripping, like most buckets had over the last hundred years or more.

'And do you know, Alfred, my dad has invented a giant magnet to draw enemy planes out of the skies?'

This set Alfred wondering how His Majesty's doctor had passed this man fit for service. Perhaps he had good teeth? It was,

The drill course at Uxbridge (Tubby is in the back row, right)

however, only a matter of time before Sam was released to carry out his inventions in private life.

Drilling was by Corporal Denton, a dedicated Eastender with black curly hair and a pleasant smile, who passed on his words of command firmly and diligently to the raw recruits.

One, a fresh-faced, young fat boy, who was very much over-mothered, soon became known as 'Tubby'. He was for ever bringing down his right foot when all the rest of the sprogs were bringing down their left. For two months he tried strenuously to correct this misdemeanour. You could almost see the smug smile of satisfaction on the rare occasions when that left foot was obeying mental orders to come down just right. But no, the right foot was always master. Nor could poor old Tubby lay out his kit correctly for inspection, but he never lost his temper. He was always a trier, but the new medical officer was a better one, for he finally got Tubby released from His Majesty's services.

The sprogs were now beginning to take shape, but one called Ron never seemed to wash. The corporal noticed his lack of 'ablutions' and ordered some men to gather up Ron and take him to the baths. They were ordered to scrub him down with a hard-bristled brush. Ron broke away from the men and rushed around the parade ground naked. Eventually he was captured and weeks of body odour were scrubbed off. This had a profound effect on Ron, he got to like soap and water so much that at every available opportunity he would go for a bath.

It was time for the great church parade and the following day would be passing-out day for all the men. It was Tubby's last great effort, with Herculean strength of character he put all his efforts into this occasion. He had actually learned the art of creasing his trousers by turning them inside out, running down the seam of his trousers with soap and water, and then turning them back and ironing them. He was duly proud of his achievement and he now started to don his immaculate uniform, but something seemed amiss, his trousers were creased crosswise. Tubby had run the iron down the joining seams of his trousers. As he stood there looking at himself he resembled a well-fed matelot on a month's leave.

'You'll have to miss the parade,' said Alfred, 'hide under the table.'

Tubby rolled himself under the ironing table and the ironing blanket was draped over and down the sides. Tubby was secure from prying eyes. There was a bit of scuffling and someone shouted, 'Eh up, McGee's coming.'

Just then Tubby noticed a pair of polished boots peeping under the blanket, and whispered, 'Come under here mate, that silly sod McGee won't find you under here.'

A slight pause, then the edge of the blanket was raised with the aid of a warrant officer's yardstick: 'So, the silly sod won't find you, eh! Come out me lad, you're on jankers,' said McGee.

The following day was the passing-out parade, minus Tubby, of course. After three months of square bashing, Alfred's squad looked fit to win a world-war battle on its own.

But first they were to have their barrack room checked by WO McGee to ascertain that all equipment was present and correct. McGee came bouncing back into the room of Cut Block. 'Now me lads, do yer see what's missing?'

The duty corporal replied, 'Just two scrubbing brushes, sir.'

In a commanding voice and turning to the men, McGee said, 'Now, me lads, do yer see you've got to scrounge two scrubbing brushes – do yer see? Now that's not stealing, is it Barker?'

Alfred realised he was being addressed. 'Oh yes, it is stealing, sir.'

All went quiet after this brave remark; then loud guffaws followed from the men.

'Be quiet!' said McGee, 'Barker is only telling the truth, so he can find the two missing brushes.' McGee bounced out knowing that within the hour of his return all would be well.

Spot on the hour McGee returned. 'Well, Barker, all's well I see, you've found the two brushes. Where did you find them?'

'In the room next door, sir.'

'You silly young sod,' shouted McGee, 'I'm in charge of all Cut Block and now they'll be short of brushes.'

It was now time to muster for the great passing-out parade: blazing cap badges and tunic buttons, white ceremonial belts, packs and other military accoutrements.

They formed up in fours and were marched across the parade ground towards the open road, with bands blasting forth military marches. Alfred felt tall and proud; being a tall man he was usually in the leading file of men. Suddenly a familiar voice thundered across the parade ground. 'That man on the left of the leading file of men, you're marching like a pregnant duck.'

Alfred began to smile at this remark, but then the truth suddenly dawned upon him, that he was the man in question. He immediately moderated his goose-like step.

They were sent to Henlow to finish their training and were then sorted into small groups for dispatch to various RAF stations throughout the UK.

2

Posted to Leconfield

ALFRED was eventually to find himself posted to Leconfield where there was a squadron of Handley Page Heyford bombers with Kestrel engines. Their maximum speed was 142 mph and as he watched them take off from the runway they reminded him of fat geese running as hard as they could to gather speed for take off. When fully loaded, with a 3,500 lb bomb load, the effort seemed too much for the planes.

After a short stay at Leconfield as a military policeman he was dispatched, in July 1937, to Hendon. Here he was involved in lining the route for George VI's Coronation, and was also to take part in the last air display of military planes from Hendon.

The display area was showing the old workhorse – the Airspeed Oxford, in later days known as the Ox Box when she saw service in Canada, Australia, Rhodesia, New Zealand and the Middle East.

There were Whitleys, and 101 squadron with their Overstrands, still classed as a first-line bomber. The famous Anson, the first plane to have a retractable undercarriage, which was operated by turning a winding gear by hand. Hawker Harts; the short-nosed Blenheim was a more modern plane; the Hendon night bomber and the Fairey Battle (which proved later to be under-gunned). No. 66 Squadron of Duxford were there with their Gauntlet bi-planes, which were still front-line fighters and still in their silver colours, the order of the day, as they were more easily discovered if force landed in wild areas.

The Hawker Fury gave a great display and number 13 Squadron displayed their Hectors. Also the Hawker Henleys, the Miles Master training aircraft and the Wellington bomber (one of the most modern and successful aircraft of the day with its geodedic construction). And the Wellesley of world-long-distance fame. The Vickers Virginia was there for its last public display and the Handley Page Hampton with the wonderful speed of 265 mph.

The Hurricane and Spitfire were still on the secret list and were not in service yet. Alfred felt it a great shame that some of the wonderful flying boats of the era could not be shown at inland bases. The Germans were there in number, and were probably having a field day in reviewing many of the older-type planes and seeing how few new ones were on show. Alfred felt that he was in the centre of things at Hendon.

One day he was asked if he would care to act as a rear gunner in a flight of Hawker Hinds which were about to give a bombing

The Wellesley – the world's long distance record holder – in the Western Desert

display over a mock harbour and ship in the centre of the drome. Donning flying helmet, goggles and flying jacket, he promptly took up his position in the rear cockpit. On taking off Alfred was surprised to find himself in the leading plane of the flight. As they rose to take up formation Alfred noticed that a Hind was flying on the starboard side. In the gunner's cockpit was a cameraman cranking his hand-turned camera. Alfred was to be a film star and the picture was to be called *Under the Shadow of the Wings*.

Whether it was the threat of war, or the shame of showing our old aircraft to the Germans, the film was later cancelled and Alfred was not to be a great film star after all.

The men, drawn from RAF units around the country, were billeted in tents opposite the newly formed Hendon Police College. Among them were identical twins, who found it very convenient to stand in for one another on duty patrols. The duty MPs could never tell the difference between the two.

Alfred and his mate, Doug, found themselves on general duties in the Mess Marquee. They were detailed for work in the store tent where the rations were kept. They came across a large bag of sugar partly hidden behind some cardboard boxes. They inquired of the sergeant cook about this bag of sugar. 'Put that one aside, lads, that's for the warrant officer,' he told them.

The warrant officer was commonly known as 'shitty arse' by the men. Doug waited for the sergeant to disappear and then turned to Alfred. 'We're on bloody rations and that sod of a WO can pinch all that sugar off us. I'll soon fix him.'

From some unknown source he eventually returned with a large packet of Epsom salts and nonchalantly started to mix it with the sugar. 'That should do the trick, Alfred. I bet that WO will have no more trouble with constipation after a dose of that mixture.' And that's how he acquired the name 'shitty arse'.

In due course Alfred and the rest of the men were returned to their respective units. Alfred returned to Leconfield and was re-mustered to go on a fitters-mate course at Manston. These courses were well organised to get the maximum training in the shortest possible time. Trained men were urgently needed in the now expanding air force.

After hammering, chiselling and measuring and learning about the march of aero engines, the course was nearing completion. The men were almost Riggers and Mechanics, in theory. It was now time for a little relaxation in the old wooden stove-heated huts of Manston.

On Saturday evening the men began preparing for going out to wherever took their fancy. While some of the men were listening to the rantings and raving of Herr Hitler on the news items, AC Clewes had heated up some water on the top of the stove with a view to having a shave. 'I do hate shaving,' said he, as he turned to AC Lofty Lowe.

'No further trouble, mate, I'll shave you,' replied Lofty.

He thereupon produced a deadly looking cut-throat razor and

The Mechanics' course at Henlow, 1937

badger-haired shaving brush. Professionally. he placed a clean towel around AC Clewes's neck and started to lather his face as far up as his forehead.

'What the hell do you think you're doing, Lofty?'

'Oh shut up and sit still, I've got to do something while the water hots up haven't I?

The stove by this time was almost red-hot and AC Clewes's knees were almost on fire.

'I'm ready to shave you now,' said Lofty, as he brandished the deadly looking cut-throat around Clewes's head and face.

Watching the event with some uncontrolled amusement, Alfred suddenly whispered to Lofty, 'Dip your razor into the hot water, let it cool just a bit, then draw the back of it across his neck.'

Action was instantaneous, Clewes sprang two and a half feet into the air and, clutching his burning throat shouted, 'He's cut me throat, he's cut me throat, the bastard's cut me throat.'

He removed his clasped left hand to look at his saturated blood-stained fist, but his unbelieving eyes could not discern any blood.

He re-grasped his throat with his right hand. Surely that would be covered in blood, but no, there was no sign of blood anywhere. The puzzlement on his face was amazing to behold, for he could still feel the imaginary searing entry of the blade on his throat. Yet the laughing, tear-stained faces of his compatriots denied his worst thoughts.

'You bastard, Lofty, I'll get you for this! That sod Barker, I heard him whispering to you, he's for it as well.'

With a bound he jumped on Lofty's back and brought him to the ground and they seemed to get mixed up with the strip of carpet on the floor. With the help of his mate, he rolled Lofty up in the carpet, with his head sticking out one end and his feet out the other. They then tied a rope around the human parcel and, picking him up in the carpet, they deposited him on the steps of the warrant officer's hut.

All the occupants of the men's hut suffered jankers after that episode.

They were all now due to finish their technical training at

Henlow. This was a course as flight mechanics and riggers. At Henlow they were still training parachute jumping on the Vickers Virginia bi-plane by standing on the wing tip and pulling the rip-cord, hoping that the parachute would not become entangled on the tail plane.

Henlow's new wing, including the cookhouse, was now fully occupied by men of the RAF expansion programme. The sudden arrival of so many men caused the cooks to use new cooking utensils which they hastily dipped into soda water and such like before cooking with them.

Alfred, Lofty, Lowe and mates went into town that evening for a few drinks and sing-song in the local pubs. When walking with not a care in the world down the main street, they suddenly had to quicken their paces. The need to find a loo was suddenly getting very urgent but, as ever on these occasions, things seemed to be on the secret list. They now had to start running; in the distance they spied several people coming out of an entrance, who were surreptitiously glancing down at their fronts, a sure sign of checking to see if they were properly re-adjusted in dress.

Alfred and Lofty Lowe, being good cross-country runners, were the first there; without looking left or right they dived inside only to be greeted with screams – they were in the ladies' loo. Nothing could deter them now, things were very urgent. Underpants were discarded in waste baskets, and they quickly returned to camp, fearful of even passing wind.

Within the next few days they had never experienced so much activity. After filing and chiselling and studying and writing, the flight mechanics' and riggers' course went ahead.

At lunch time the men knocked off work to go to the nice new cookhouse with the modern equipment and elaborate cooking arrangements. The smell of fish cooking greeted their nostrils. There was also the additional smell which made the men's nostrils twitch.

Lofty turned to Alfred and said, 'That bloody fish has got a queer smell about it, Alfred.'

While they were in the queue they noticed that those who were served kept picking up their plates and smelling the fish.

Suddenly the orderly sergeant, followed by a new sprog of an officer entered. The orderly officer asked, 'Any complaints?'

Up sprang an irate airman by a table close to the orderly officer and shouted, 'Yes, this.' Through the air came a stinking fish and it caught the officer full in the face. For a few seconds there was pandemonium, then deathly silence followed, as the enormity of the situation dawned. The orderly sergeant eventually came to life and shouted, 'Fall in two men, march that man to the guard room.'

When Lofty's and Alfred's turn came to be served, all further issue of stinking fish was suspended.

Several more days of studying and working on test jobs and the course on Rolls-Royce Kestrel engines manufactured at Alfred's home town of Derby followed. He wondered if those two young men from Parker's garage in Siddals Road had finally joined Rolls-Royce as mechanics.

Alfred was musing on this as he strolled by the grass verge towards the parade ground. Suddenly he noticed a mud-stained football; half-consciously he stepped back apace and with skill gave it a fancy touch with his toe. The reaction was instantaneous, not with the ball but with Alfred's foot. A thousand needles seemed to penetrate his big toe. The ball stood in exactly the same spot and Alfred viewed it with consternation, suddenly realising it was made of iron. It looked like the round weight off a yardarm scales and it was probably placed there purposely.

His mates were some way off and walking towards him. He hobbled down the road and turning round shouted, 'Kick that ball back, mate.' Of all things it was poor old Clewes again. Alfred wished he'd never uttered those words, but it was too late. Clewes, like a professional, stepped back, gave a light leap forward and a little gentler than usual, kicked. Thank God for that, thought Alfred. He should not have played such a dirty trick on this same man for a second time.

There was a resounding dull thud, and then a muffled ring from the iron ball. Clewes had one foot arrested in mid-air from the rebound of the kick. He began to hop about with his one good foot; the throbbing stabs of pain refused to let his other foot come to earth.

'You rotten bastard, Barker, you knew that ball was made of iron.'

'Not till after I'd kicked it,' replied Alfred.

Although Alfred tried to make it up with Clewes later on, he was never successful.

As the passing-out day came Alfred now had 'superior' marked on his documents: he was now AC First Class Flight Mechanic. His next move, in 1938, was to 66 Squadron RAF Duxford. AC Doug Eaton went with him as a rigger. Nos. 19 and 66 Squadrons were part of No. 12 fighter group for the defence of North London.

Alfred was billeted to Block 13 Room 3. It struck him as strange that the number 13 would crop up so often throughout his RAF career.

The ground crew organisation was the ex-Halton apprentices of fitter I for engines and airframes, with the aid of a fitter's mate and auxiliary crews. Now Alfred, as a flight mechanic, and Doug Eaton, as the rigger, were the first pair of this new ground crew structure to be tried out at Duxford on 66 Squadron.

For a while the ex-Halton boys tried to take a rise out of these lads, but as time went on they were gladly accepted as part of the team.

In 1938, with the threat of war ever nearer, the front-line fighters of Duxford were still in the silver-painted Gloster Gauntlets, with a speed of 230 mph, and with two machine guns.

The senior NCOs were Flight Sergeant Mitchell and Sergeant Chapman, in charge of Alfred's flight. Both were well liked, except when the former passed wind while in the adjoining office to the adjutant. Flight Sergeant Mitchell's consumption of Guinness in his copious belly turned into a deadly gas overnight; the resulting outlet produced the most deadly smell.

The adjutant would rush out gasping for fresh air and shouting, 'You stinking devil, Mitchell.' With a mischievous grin on his face, Mitchell remarked, 'It's the only time I can shift you out of your office, sir.'

The powers that be gradually realised that war could become a possibility, so the order went out to transform the silver clad

Gauntlets and Gladiators into wartime colours of camouflage. Officers and men were provided with brushes and dope to set about the task. Work went on from dawn to late night.

After hearing the ranting and ravings of Hitler on the wireless news, the order went out that everything was now of immediate action.

As Alfred glanced up at the officers' protruding shoes over the edge of the main planes he was surprised at the number of worn-out shoes, many with holes in the soles. Young officers' pay was not sufficient to pay for messing fees and uniform. But their pay structure was soon to be altered to attract more young men to join the RAF.

The order now went out to belt up all the available rounds of ammunition for the guns of the planes. Some 3–500,000 rounds of ammunition was belted up, mainly by every available man by hand. In consequence of which there were many sore fingers.

The 1936 Spitfire, K5054
(reproduced by permission of Rolls-Royce plc)

More ammunition was sent for, but none was available from any source; the grimness of the situation was beginning to filter down to the ranks.

The Bessemer hangars, untouched for years, were now surrounded by men with brushes and dope to camouflage them. Churchill's constant warnings to the nation were gradually being taken notice of, albeit reluctantly by some of the leaders.

The first Spitfire prototype flew from Southampton Airport in 1936. Now suddenly in August 1938 the very first Mark I Spitfire and the third production machine to be issued to the RAF landed at Duxford. It was Mark I K9789 and it was quickly taken into the hangar of 19 Squadron.

Shortly afterwards, 66 Squadron began to get issued with these beautiful new monoplanes. After the slow but reliable bi-planes, a new world of aviation was opened up to the personnel. Pilots, fitters, riggers, electricians, wireless operators and amourers and other men surrounded the planes, extolling the virtues of this or that, according to their trades.

Alfred's Spitfire, with Lieutenant Sergeant Chapman

Unstoppable, Hitler was now causing great consternation to world leaders, and particularly to the RAF, for Germany was proving that aircraft would play a more formidable role in future events.

England's leaders were still relying on running the world's greatest empire's outposts with old-type bi-planes, dropping odd bombs here and there on dissident tribesmen's huts, but warning them first of the impending danger.

Peace had been maintained mainly by trade, with the vast industrial revolution opening up new routes across great continents. We formed the world's first air-postal service, mainly with the long-distance flying boats.

In early June 1938, the first Spitfires, with two-bladed wooden propellers instead of the three-bladed metal props of variable pitch, were rushed out to the defence squadrons. Lead weights were fitted to the sides of the engine's mountings to even up the weight of the missing heavier variable pitch units. Eight machine guns and 355 mph and its streamlined, fish-shaped body made this a formidable plane.

The pilots were now very keen to fly them; they had been used to the lightweight bi-planes, almost floating down to earth on landing. Now suddenly they were to fly a heavier and much faster-landing monoplane. Quite a few pilots landed nose-heavy, breaking off the tips of the wooden blades. This was a blessing in disguise, for it was quicker and cheaper to replace a two-bladed wooden propeller and it caused much less damage to the plane.

The ground crews also found their new monoplane different from the old bi-planes. When running up to full throttle to test the magnetoes, the fitters were instructed to see that a man's weight was on the tail plane to stop it lifting into flying position. Doug Eaton, Alfred's rigger, was one day supposed to be safely ensconced on the tail plane. Alfred, testing the magnetoes, pushing forward the throttle lever, found the engine responded to around 2,000 revs per minute. Suddenly he noticed the technical officer by the Bessemer hangar door waving his arms for Alfred to throttle down the engine. He then noticed he had been in flying position and Doug Eaton was lying on the ground; he had slipped off the tail of the plane.

Intensified flying tests and manoeuvres were now the order of the day. The American Tomahawk with its Allison engine was lined up against our Spitfires ready for take off; our Spitfires were in the air before the Tomahawks had reached the end of the runway. The Allison engine was no match at that time against the Merlin II engine. The early Spitfires developed a serious blow-back into the induction manifold which should have been rectified at Rolls-Royce. Owing to urgency of delivery to the squadron, this had not been done.

The RAF could ill afford to have these planes unserviceable at this critical stage of world affairs. Two engineers from Rolls-Royce in Derby were sent to Duxford to oversee the modifications which necessitated the dismantling of the induction manifold. A gauze filter was then fitted securely with a number of BA nuts and bolts. The whole replaced and the engines re-timed, they were then checked by Rolls-Royce engineers.

Alfred was completing the work on his Spitfire late into the night, when to his surprise he found the two Rolls-Royce engineers were the very same men from Parker's garage in Siddals Road, Derby.

The work went on night and day with very little sleep for the men. It was fortunate that at his particular time a flame-trap had been designed for the Merlin Marine Motor Torpedo boat, and this was the type fitted to the early RAF Merlin engines. There was very little time off for sleeping but all the men were ready and very keen for anything that might be thrown at them in the coming months. The early carefree days of service life were beginning to take the form of long, slogging days and nights with the constant worry about the condition of our planes and equipment.

There were little incidents which provided light relief, however, such as when Alfred was pointing out to the technical sergeant a small teething trouble of the early Spitfire.

There was a Glicol leak in the rubber connection of the radiator. This necessitated the sergeant putting his head into the rear of the radiator to inspect the trouble. While he was doing this, a young pilot was showing another the cockpit controls. He operated the radiator shutter flaps and they flew down with terrific force, hit the sergeant on the back of the head and pinned him inside the radiator.

The eventual release of the sergeant's head also resulted in the release of a pent-up string of abuse. There were adjectives Alfred hadn't heard of before and the startled young pilot was full of apologies.

Alfred's earliest Spitfire I K9490 was chosen to do 500 hours nonstop flying; as soon as one pilot landed another one took control. The Merlin engine stood the test well, but a few of the rivets in the wings gave way, so stronger rivets formed the modifications in future Spitfires.

The plane was then flown to Farnborough to assess the condition of frame and engine. When it came back Alfred was amazed to see a hole had been cut in the fuselage of the plane just rear of the pilot. A carbon-pile had been fitted which consisted of several carbon capsules mounted on a platform with wires attached. Apparently this was to test the cutting out of interference on the radio. After further tests it was then flown back to Farnborough for final checking on condition of frame, engine and radio. This aircraft later became the firm's trials aircraft and was completely stripped down for detailed inspection after its service trials at Duxford. In July 1940, it went to YOTU. Alfred and Doug Eaton, as flight mechanic and rigger, were detailed to go to Norwich to show the people their first close-up of a Spitfire, and to witness its flying capabilities. This was K9945. A clapped-out, old, dual-controlled Fairey Battle, with Alfred in the dual-control cockpit, and Doug Eaton in the confines of the bombpit, struggled to fly them to Norwich.

On landing, poor old Doug Eaton extricated himself from the narrow oil-spattered bombpit of the plane. His face was covered with sump oil from the breather; he was due immediately to go with Alfred and start up the Spitfire engine ready for the pilot to fly.

Behind the roped-off area the girls were desperately trying to hold down their clothes against the slip-stream of the Spitfire. Doug, with a grin from ear to ear of his oil-spattered face, was a sight to behold. Alfred and he were both apprehensive about flying back to Duxford in the decrepit old Fairey Battle.

Cambridge was the nearest town for 66 Squadron personnel on their occasional visits. The Fountain or Criterion pubs were their favourite places for a drink. In the Fountain the lounge was usually occupied by young men and women of the colleges. Lofty, Alfred and Doug were having a quiet drink in the bar when suddenly a gowned undergraduate entered the pub hastily and darted under the lounge counter to gain entry into the bar. Leaning on the bar he suddenly tore off his gown and facing the three men he ordered four whiskies, as if he had been with them all evening.

The lounge door suddenly burst open and another figure appeared, dressed in top hat and cape. He searched the area of the lounge and then departed.

'Thank God for that,' said our new-found friend. 'If that Buller had seen me I'd have been expelled from the college.' He then insisted on buying drink after drink until after the fifth whisky Alfred went to the outside loo. It was suddenly as if someone had hit him behind the knees and he fell down on the floor. Eventually on re-entering the bar, the trio shouted in unison, 'Good God, you look as white as a ghost, what's up with you?'

The undergraduate said, 'It's the beer you had first, not the whisky. If you have another whisky now you'll feel OK.'

There was no escaping, Alfred just had to have another whisky and sure enough it seemed to settle his stomach.

'You see that tall bloke in the lounge,' said the student, 'well, the lads have bet him he could not stand after 12 double whiskies, he's still standing and has won his £5 bet.'

On the way back to the railway station they all called at the chip shop for the inevitable paper-wrapped fish and chip supper.

The planes had not yet been placed out on dispersal points around the drome. Panic tests of quick starting and take off of the Spitfires were done from the hangar. On dummy runs of 'raiders approaching' the shout of 'man the hangar doors' brought men rushing to push the heavy sliding doors open. Planes were rushed out in double-quick time.

Doug Eaton ran and placed the battery trolley into position. Alfred ran as hard as he could go to plug in the starter-lead,

Dummy run of raiders approaching

between the mainplane and propeller; the pilot pressed his starter button, the engine spluttered into life, and before it had time to gather momentum Alfred unplugged the starting lead and dashed out to take the lead back to Doug Eaton.

Poor old Doug stood there goggle-eyed and white-faced. 'You've just come right through the prop!' said he.

It was fortunate that they were still two-bladed wooden propellers and Alfred was so quick in moving. After that episode he always made sure of following back along the mainplane before coming away from the plane.

As war seemed more certain the planes were put out on dispersal points and the mechanics started up the engine ready for the pilot to take off. And a few weeks later feverish activity ensued when the number of men on the camp jumped from 600 to 1,800, due to the influx of class C reservists.

It was at this time that Alfred first became aware of the radar system. We were one up on Hitler with this new invention. We could tell when his planes were taking off across the Channel and follow their course to our shores. The radar with our Hurricanes and Spitfires was instrumental in saving us from invasion in later days.

Intensified flying tests and manoeuvres were now the order of the day. Alfred's flight of 66 Squadron was dispatched to King's Lynn. The gun emplacements of the Spitfires were fitted out with cameras; they showed up the wonderful fire-power against the mock invaders of the Eastern shores.

Sergeant Parker, Alfred and a civilian driver went on a loaded Queen Mary Articulator to King's Lynn. The Spitfires on manoeuvres showed up several faults, later to be modified. One was the starvation of fuel with the carburettor, in later times to be fitted with a diaphragm to counteract the trouble.

On the return trip to Duxford, Sergeant Parker took over the driving of the vehicle, contrary to orders. He was passing some cyclists and drew in sharply to avoid an oncoming agricultural lorry loaded with bags of cattle food. The articulated front load of equipment caught the bags of cattle feed and lacerated them from front to rear of the lorry.

Farmers returning from the local market stopped and accused

the RAF men of negligence, as the bags emptied their contents on to the road. They were well aware that no claims could be made against the Crown for compensation in those days.

Sergeant Parker now decided that his driving skills were not up to standard and the civilian driver resumed his position in the driving seat. Parker went to wind the huge starting handle, the engine back-fired, then burst into life. Alfred took up position in the middle seat. After a short while he noticed the sergeant holding his arm – his face was ashen white. 'Let's have a look at your arm, Serg,' said Alfred.

He thought the man was going to faint. When the sergeant took his hand away from his right arm, Alfred could see the bone of the forearm was almost protruding through the skin.

'Drive to the nearest hospital,' said leading aircraftman Barker, for from now on he was in control and would be responsible for all future activity. On reaching Royston Hospital Alfred went in with the injured sergeant. When he returned to the Queen Mary Articulator the civilian driver was finishing a bottle of Red Biddy.

Alfred grabbed the bottle. 'Give me that bottle, mate, you're not fit to drive.'

'Sod you, mate, I'm going in the pub for a drink.' Off went the inebriated driver, grabbing the briefcase with all the form 700s and other documents which would have held vital evidence of the performance of our aircraft should it fall into enemy hands. Alfred followed the driver, who was brandishing the briefcase and shouting, 'Anyone want to buy a bag full of secrets?'

The seated occupants in the pub looked on in dumb silence while Alfred snatched the case and pulled the driver back to the vehicle. Then he took over the driving back to Duxford camp, where the RAF MPs were awaiting them at the guard room.

A court of inquiry ensued and Alfred, who was afraid of getting Sergeant Parker into further trouble, refrained from answering vital questions. He was threatened with a charge. But on pointing out that from the moment he was in charge he had made sure that all was safely delivered back to camp, the charges against him were dropped. Later the civilian driver was relieved of his duties and Sergeant Parker, an ill man at the time, died a few years later.

The memory of those incidents came flooding back years later when Alfred visited Duxford.

The regulars were now tented out around the drome on dispersal points. They worked from 3 a.m. to 11 p.m. nonstop for a week, running up the engines of the Spitfires every now and then to keep the engines warm.

Scrambles were coming thick and fast; some of them were dummy runs to keep everyone on the alert. Radar in its infancy was being tested out.

Food at the base was brought over from the cookhouse in containers, potatoes with the jackets on, mashed up with whatever the over-stretched cooks could muster. This was eaten in an old barn which had been commandeered from a neighbouring farmer. The wind blew through the many gaps in the woodwork, sending clouds of chaff to mix with the food.

Teatime was cut out and so was the sweet for dinner. The canteen across at camp was mainly out of bounds, but one could still get watered-down beer.

The spirits of the men were bruised but the resolve was there to face what was to come.

The planes were ever ready on dispersal points; the pilots all keyed up for action and trenches were dug already around the perimeter. Suddenly on 3 September 1939, Chamberlain gave his momentous speech.

'We are now at war.' Those words emblazoned themselves on the keen young men's minds.

As Alfred looked about him at the fresh-faced youngsters, from the higher homes of the land to those from humbler beginnings, and to the many young men from the universities who had cut short their careers, all keen to serve their country, he wondered what their future would be, if any, in the coming years of conflict.

Part of the answer was soon to arrive with another radar warning of enemy aircraft approaching in number. The Spitfires' took off, the ground crews waiting anxiously for their return, and particularly for the Spitfire that they maintained.

Odd planes came and circled the drome to land but one was in trouble. Probably he had used up all his fuel. He flew low over some trees around the perimeter of the Duxford landing grounds, hit the tops of the trees and cut a pattern in the shape of the dihedral of the plane's wings through the top branches of the trees. Pilot Officer Patan, a pleasant, fresh-faced and well liked young man, was to be the first casualty of 66 Squadron at war.

There was now a warning of spies in the vicinity, then the message that some other Spitfire squadron had shot down two of our Hurricanes in mistake. At this period of time the German Fokker Wolf 190 was better than the first Spitfires.

A new NCO was posted to the squadron, who was a class C reservist recently recalled for service. He was without any experience of modern aircraft yet was put in charge of regulars who were trained and experienced on the then most modern planes.

In 1939 the strength of our aircraft at home was 1,476 and 435 overseas, the total strength of the personnel was 118,000 and 68,000 reservists. Germany had some 3,600 first-line aircraft with 500,000 personnel and around 500,000 on anti-aircraft duties.

The navy was ill-equipped with defence, in the fact that the torpedo bomber of coastal command with gunpower of one forward and one aft gun of the Vildebeest was their only torpedo bomber. Many of the type of planes that Alfred had seen at the Hendon display of 1937 were still in front-line service.

3

Posted to 219 Squadron

ON 5th October 1939, No 219 Squadron of Blenheims was about to be formed. Alfred was posted there as a leading aircraftsman with exceptional special recommendations on his documents. Catterick RAF camp was the destination. His new commanding officer was Wing Commander R. L. R. Atcherley who was to start this new squadron. He was the very man who had won the King's Cup Air Race in a Gloster Grebe in 1926, and later the Schneider Trophy in a Supermarine S6 at 331.6 mph. This was the plane that Alfred had seen on show at the Tramway Depot in Derby.

Wing Commander Atcherley liked to be called Batchy Atchy. He was quite famous for his stunt displays. He had visited America and dressed in hunting pink, using his plane like a bucking horse over jumps. At that period he also clocked up the most flying hours of any pilot in the RAF. He had a twin brother (later lost in a Meteor while on a flight from the Canal zone to Cyprus). Both brothers had decided to join the RAF at the same time; David was rejected on account of kidney trouble and Richard on eyesight defect. But within two months they both tried again; with a little help from them, the doctor seemed to get mixed up. They were both duly passed as fit for the RAF.

This was the period of the rotary-engined bi-plane when Richard graduated from Cranwell in 1922 to join No. 29 squadron on Sopwith Snipe bi-planes. While a test pilot at

Farnborough he developed the system of air-to-air refuelling. In 1942 he was shot down and rescued from the Channel while flying a Spitfire from Henley. He commanded 211 Group of the Desert Air Force in the Middle East and was later at the HQ of Allied Expeditionary Air Force where he adapted the successful air tactics of the Middle East for the invasion of Europe.

Now at Catterick, this Wing Commander, with his charismatic and purposeful character, ordered his new personnel on to the parade ground. It was freezing cold, but Batchy was going to prove the staying powers of his new troops. For over an hour the men were made to stand on parade, with the occasional varied words of command to relieve the monotony. On further inspection of the men, Batchy and his henchmen eventually stood before Alfred.

'You, leading aircraftsman, your greatcoat is in a disgusting state, get a new one.'

'I've already tried, sir, there is none in the stores. I had to use my greatcoat as a pillow when we lived in tents on the Spitfire squadron.'

'When I want your life's history, I'll ask for it, my lad.'

But Alfred had noticed a lifting of the eyebrows in approval when he had mentioned Spitfire squadron. Turning to the sergeant, Batchy said, 'See that this man gets a new greatcoat, Sergeant.'

Alfred was senior to many of the new men on the squadron, so Batchy, probably remembering the mention of the Spitfire squadron, chose him as his personal mechanic and Glyn Williams as the rigger on his Magister aircraft.

'Start it, Barker. I want to fly it.' It was 7.30 in the morning and the start of one of the coldest winters.

'But I've not done the daily inspection, sir. I don't even know how much petrol is in the tank, sir.'

'Who am I?' demanded Batchy.

'The commanding officer, sir,' replied Alfred.

'Then you'll take an order from me, start it up.'

This was easier said than done, for the plane had stood outside the hangar in the freezing cold air. Alfred and Glyn obtained a blow lamp, hotted up two house-bricks and placed them on the induction manifold of the engine. Then when the engine was turned, it quickly burst into life.

Batchy Atcherley immediately got into the cockpit and took off.

He did the most outrageous stunts, the plane seeming to obey every daring whim of this maniac pilot. He came into a pretence landing with one wing tip touching the ground and one wheel, then he would switch over to the other side with the starboard wing tip and wheel just touching the ground. Then he would jump the plane into the air and down again. The riggers were not very pleased with this madman when they had to repair the wing tips of the plane.

In his desire to get the squadron operational, Batchy borrowed or purloined any old Blenheim that was to be had for the asking, or even demanded, by this forceful character. He started to train pilots in any type of plane that could be scrounged. Many of the would-be-flyers were new from the flying schools with the minimum of experience but he made them fly in all sorts of weather. Some of them were terrified after trying to land at night with Batchy's dimmed lighting system.

The ground crews had not yet been issued with full toolboxes and Alfred made screwdrivers out of old flying wires.

One day, when an old Blenheim acquired from some dubious source came in to land, the pilot found that it had no serviceable air brakes. It ran out of control on to the main Catterick road, narrowly missing an armoured convoy. Alfred and crew were on guard after slewing it round on to the grass verge.

Batchy was now experimenting with flare-path techniques to try and cut out the tell-tale flare path lights – later to be known and adopted throughout the RAF as the DREM lighting system. Pilots were made to fly at night and then to try and land with these dimmed flares. If a pilot was afraid to land, Batchy would be out there on the drome firing red Very lights to show them the landing strip.

When starting up, the old Blenheim often had a blow-back in the induction system; a fire would start and one had to run and stuff a field-service cap into the induction mouth to smother the fire. Alfred always maintained that was what the field service cap was invented for; it was a useless article for headwear at any rate.

In November of 1939, surprise, surprise, three Blenheims were received that were actually designated to 219 Squadron. Let us give thanks to the Phoney War at this stage.

On the 14th a Magister crashed and killed the pilot; on the 18th, 18 Hawker Harts visited the drome for refuelling – they were on their way to Renfrew. On the 28th, Alfred's Blenheim No. 8686 crashed into the top of a tree on the perimeter of the drome. The two propellers, still turning madly, broke off the engines and screwed themselves into the bowels of the earth. The young terrified pilot was thrown through the cockpit window but escaped injury.

The winter of 1939 proved very severe, a heavy blanket of snow lay over the drome, cutting out flying, or so everybody thought. But not Batchy Atchy, for he could even conquer the elements. He managed to persuade the powers that be at Catterick army camp to loan him around 3,000 soldiers. As they came marching on to the drome, knee-deep in snow with shovels and spades at the ready, they resembled a film being enacted on an Everest expedition.

A landing strip was soon made clear, training of pilots was resumed. From some unknown source, Batchy had acquired a barrel of beer. This was placed in the hangar for working ground crew; then Batchy organised the pilots in mid-air to sing carols as they were flying and this was relayed to the airmen in the hangar.

The Germans started to send in planes at night to avoid our fighters. Batchy responded by going up in a Blenheim to try and intercept them when they were in the area.

One night Alfred had a nightmare – his father was very ill and about to die. The next morning the adjutant sent for him and said that he had a telegram from Alfred's mother that his father was seriously ill. A week's leave was granted. Alfred arrived at Derby LMS late at night and had to walk the five miles to the farm. He was stopped on the way by a cycling policeman who was not risking spies being disguised as airmen in his area.

On the farm he found that the army had invaded the house

field, there were billets, anti-aircraft guns, a pill-box and an air-raid shelter.

Within the week Alfred's father died. But previous to this he had said, 'England is a lovely country, fight for it, you've all been good sons and daughters.'

On returning to Catterick Alfred found himself on duty crew again when fifteen Hawker Harts visited the drome for refuelling. The RAF was moving its older type aircraft into position ready for the threatened invasion of our little island. A Spitfire landed for refuelling and he felt reassured that it had a variable pitch propeller, not the two-bladed wooden props of 66 Squadron days. Perhaps Beaverbrook was hurrying forward production in our factories? An American Lockheed then landed. Alfred wondered how long it would be before America entered the war on our side.

In January the papers informed us that a German plane had been shot down on the east coast, and that 4,000 people had been killed in an earthquake in Turkey. To the people reading this, it seemed to be an incredible amount of people to die at once. Thank goodness the phoney war was still with us, as this figure would appear infinitesimal in a few years' time.

Russia had now sent in 1,000 tanks against Finland and the Irish Free State had found many tons of ammunition stored away. The Germans were threatening Sweden and Switzerland if France and Great Britain sent help to Finland. General Goering took over complete control of economics, and Hore-Belisha threatened to resign as he favoured helping the Finns.

4

Posted to 16 Army Co-operation Squadron

ON 25 January 1940 Alfred was called into the office and was told that he was to be posted to 16 Army Co-operation Squadron on Lysanders to join the Expeditionary Force in France. No. 16 Squadron was the first to be issued with these monoplanes in 1938. So Alfred's sojourn with Batchy Atcherley was about to end, but he gave Alfred a Superior Special Recommendation on his documents. Later in his RAF career these recommendations made little difference to Alfred's status. But Batchy Atcherley was to be an Air Marshal and inventor of the Drem Lighting System. His title eventually was Air Marshal Sir Richard Atcherley KBE, CB, AFC.

No. 16 Squadron at Old Sarum had been the first to be issued with Lysander monoplanes, a two-seat Army Co-operation plane used for artillery spotting and reconnaissance. Their speed was 229 mph, with a range of 600 miles and a bomb load around 855 lb, two forward guns and a twin 0.303 manual turret in the rear cockpit.

At Old Sarum Alfred met an old friend, Bill Brennan from 66 Squadron. The powers that be seemed not quite sure what to do with 16 Squadron, so they were moved to Hawkinge. The billets there were not allowed any heating and it was bitterly cold. After years of RAF uniforms around them, Alfred and Bill Brennan felt

16 Army Co-operation group ready to be posted to France

strange with khaki army-uniformed air crew and RAF blue-uniformed ground crews. Everything was suddenly hush, hush, on the squadron until one man, on entering the hangar, saw one of the Lysanders with what he thought was a swastika being painted on the tail fin. He then realised that it was the wrong way round, it was actually the Finnish emblem.

The men were then ordered to go to the clothing store to gather overseas kit for an expedition. This consisted of only one item – a leather jerkin. Thank goodness intervention in Finland against Russia was cancelled, along with Hore-Belisha's later resignation; all was now activity to pack for a different centre of war, namely France.

In the papers it now said that India was to modernise the RAF over there with squadrons of Blenheims and Lysanders. Alfred thought 'God help the British Empire', for he had worked on Gladiators, then Spitfires, then Blenheims. He had flown in a Fairey Battle, with a top speed of 240 mph, a range of 1,050 miles and a bomb load of 1,000 lb, but it proved to be under-powered. Ten of these squadrons were in the expeditionary force in France. The one forward gun and one rear gun were no defence against the German fighters.

Now Alfred was on Lysanders he was invited to fly with a pilot on testing the manoeuvrability of the plane. After two hours' flying time, he was very impressed with its manoeuvring but not with its speed. He could not understand why the powers that be had allowed production to go forward with a plane with fixed undercarriage, and two tiny wing fins attached to them to carry small bombs. It was all evasive action against the German fighter of Messerschmitts and Junkers 88. Praise must go to the pilots who did wonderful work with them in later times.

The men now boarded the ship at Southampton docks; fast Navy boats were constantly on patrol against any enemy submarines that may have been in the area. The threat of being torpedoed was very great. Eventually, they landed unharmed at Cherbourg, where they were loaded into second-rate rail carriages with tin cans as loos. They travelled during the night to arrive at Glissy airport. Alfred served on C flight on 16 Squadron. After regrouping, 16 Squadron was then sent to Bertangles where the landing ground was surrounded by woods and a road running through. Spaces were cut into the corner of the woods, the plane pushed in, then camouflaged with the brushwood.

During this process an amusing incident occurred. The men were constantly being warned of the presence of German parachutists. LAC Lawes and other airmen were putting the final touches to complete the camouflage when suddenly out shot a German parachutist. The airmen took aim with rifles but the German turned out to be a startled young deer; he was very lucky to be able to gallop freely off.

Tents were erected in the woods; all endeavour at this stage of the early days of the war seemed to be to hide from the enemy or attempt to fool them. Nerves were kept constantly on edge by the warnings of parachutists being dropped in the area. When on patrol duty and walking through the woods, one would suddenly hear two or three rifle shots coming from the right of the path. After recovering from the shock and finding yourself still standing, our eyes would focus on the 40-gallon petrol drums stored in the confines of the wood. The heat of the day having caused expansion of the full barrel and then the cool night air causing contraction made them give off the mighty bang.

There seemed no set plan of action, at this stage Germany held all the cards. After lying on groundsheets and covered in blankets most of the airmen developed sores under the arms and between the legs, probably caused by the humid undergrowth of the woods. This was 'cured' with the application of iodine, but it made one shout when applied between the legs.

Britain had not visualised a war being fought in France again. There wasn't ever enough transport so civilian vehicles had been requisitioned when war was first declared. There were only two bombers, four fighters, and six army co-operation squadrons sent to France. Around this period there were, apart from bomber squadrons, ten fighter squadrons, and five Lysanders squadrons of the RAF in France. Nerves were kept constantly on edge and one's thoughts nagged one on what the Germans were going to do to us – not what we were going to do to the Germans. This was soon explained to 16 Squadron with the arrival of Air Vice-Marshal Emery, a small man who constantly looked downwards as he spoke. This was probably due to the forthcoming downward lecture that he was about to give to the men:

> My men, I believe in telling you the truth of the situation that we are about to face. Your squadron is here to help try and stop the Germans from breaking through above the Maginot line. You may wonder why our forces sit here and don't go through the Belgian frontier to face the Germans, for we know precisely how many troops are facing us. The position is that we do not want to be classed as aggressors by going into Belgium. We do not want to upset American public opinion, so we have to sit here and let the Germans come through. Your squadron was destroyed in the First World War and no doubt will be destroyed in this war, for the Germans intend to form a half-moon around England. Good luck to you all.

Alfred would always remember that momentous straightforward talk, and so did many of his compatriots.

Early in February Alfred had applied to become a pilot and passed the medical examinations, but tradesmen among ground crews were in short supply. His application went no further.

The Countess of Chermont, who had her château near the camp, kindly offered the services of part of it for canteen facilities for the squadron. She often walked across the drome to talk to the men and on one occasion she told Alfred and LAC Lawes that this was the first place King Edward VIII visited on his abdication of the British throne. She said that the Germans captured the place for only three days in the First World War. She pointed out the old dugouts and trenches where old used bullets and parts of aircraft could still be found. Unfortunately, in a few months many more modern ones would be found.

At night many lights could be seen flashing signals to the enemy and much bombing would follow. It was hard to distinguish friend from foe for there seemed to be many spies in the area.

There was muddle and mayhem in February and March as

documentation for April was lost. The frustration of the occasion induced Alfred to think of the nature of the Germans, and prompted him to paint Popeye with clenched fists breaking up the German swastika on to the side of his Lysander. The pilot, Lt Reed, was perturbed when he saw the emblem and somewhat superstitious.

On 13 May, the German Panzer divisions attacked France at Sedan. They now began to bomb Amiens with Junkers and escort fighters systematically. There seemed very little intervention by our fighters. Also on 13 May Mr Churchill addressed the House of Commons for the first time.

On 17 May, Lysander L4796 was missing with F/O REB White and P/O Hamilton (AG). (I must point out that although this was an army co-operation squadron, it was registered as RAF and, although the pilots were in army uniform with army rank, they were also registered in RAF rank.)

The French army lorries towing field guns were now retreating on the road running through the camp. They were followed by the Belgians and the road was then full of refugees in horse-drawn wagons and carts, men, women and children on foot with their few belongings strapped to their backs.

The order then came through to bomb some crossroads to try and stop the Germans advancing. We were now under French command, our CO was kept busy making out reports to absolve ourselves from blame for bombing civilians caught up in the raids.

On 19 May, Lysander L4904 with F/O Walker and Corporal Baillie went missing.

Fourteen Junkers with seven fighter escorts flew over the landing ground; it was thought that they were going to land. The ground crews were ordered to hide in the woods.

Alfred and LAC Lawes, with rifles at the ready, disobeyed the order and hid behind a heap of stones with a view to shooting at any landing aircraft. There was just one machine-gun post at the corner of the wood. However, the German bombers and fighters ignored 16 Army Co-operation Squadron (or 16 RAF) and flew on to bomb Amiens, where some British fighters stood on the drome. Some of the pilots and ground crew had been killed. The

42461 Ian Dromgoole – the first New Zealand pilot
to be shot down in wartime

16 Squadron was ordered to try to ferry spare pilots over there to attempt to save our fighters.

Alfred had just loaded his kitbag into the plane ready for retreat when Lt Reed, the pilot, and F/O (Lt) Dromgoole, as the ferry pilot, ran up to the plane L4813 to take off. Alfred and LAC Lawes wished them both good luck on their dangerous mission.

They watched the plane travelling towards Amiens with the Popeye and smashed swastika emblem, and Alfred thought of Lt Reed's superstition about the emblem. Three Messerschmitts got on their tail and shot them down. Records show that Lt Reed was actually Flying Officer Andrew Patrick Reed, 25132 serving with 16 Squadron. He was 27 and, sadly, he has no known grave, but he is commemorated by name in Panel 6 of the Runnymede Memorial in Surrey. He was the son of Major-General Hamilton Reed, UC, CB, CMG, RA, of Westminster, London.

Pilot Officer Ian Dromgoole 42461 is also commemorated by name on Panel 8 of the Runnymede Memorial. He was the son of Victor Peter Dromgoole and Susan Sommerville Dromgoole of Lyttleton, Canterbury, New Zealand. It is believed he was the first New Zealander of the RAF to lose his life. He was also one of seven brothers, many of whom would later lose their lives in warfare.

The increase in traffic retreat was now causing problems; army and air force were mixed up with civilians. This mêlée was ripe for pickings with the Luftwaffe strafing them with machine-gun fire. Wireless communication was now almost non-existent; contact between units almost nil.

One day, a French army vehicle pulled up, and the driver asked for a cigarette. Alfred was about to offer his mate one, when he suddenly noticed that half his bottom jaw was missing. They had been caught by parachutists; the vehicle was full of bullet holes.

Four worn-out old British tanks were going in the opposite direction to try and stop the German infiltration. But still 16 Squadron stuck its ground. Alfred thought of his two brothers who had been fighting in France in the First World War only twenty years previously.

Armed German motor-cycle columns were now advancing rapidly towards the landing ground. The order came through to retreat; England had lost all touch with 16 Squadron. The men rapidly destroyed anything useful to the enemy, some new power-driven electric generators were buried under soil in the woods. Somebody obviously thought that at some future date they would return to find them still there.

The retreating army had commandeered some of the RAF lorries. Alfred and other NCOs, about ten men in all, were left to refuel the few remaining planes, they then had to jump on to the petrol bowser to escape the German advancing armoured columns. It was rather a precarious place to be if strafed by enemy planes, sitting on top of a large amount of petrol! Eventually they caught up with the rest of the retreating convoy which had stopped for a mug of tea at a French bivouac camp. For some inexplicable reason the senior NCOs had not yet realised the gravity of the situation. Alfred and Lawes got off the petrol bowser and went to stay with the lorries. They could not believe such rash stupidity of the NCOs who had allowed the men off the lorries. Had they not just escaped capture themselves? They felt the danger.

Suddenly a staff car screeched to a halt. Lt Clapham (records as F/O Clapham) sprang out of the vehicle in great panic. 'For God's sake, where are the men?'

'In there, sir,' said Alfred and Lawes.

'Well, for goodness sake, get them out quick; the Germans will soon be around us. Make for Rouen and Cherbourg.'

That gentleman was the saviour of many of 16 Squadron's ground crew. They eventually arrived safely at Cherbourg and were quickly loaded on to a ship for England. Much of the personnel equipment was dumped over the quayside. They were all brought together again at Lympne airport, the remaining planes dropping supplies to our beleaguered troops at Dunkerque.

By this time the Belgian army, commanded by the king, had surrendered completely and we were to evacuate near-on 409,000 troops from Dunkerque. Major-General Montgomery was to the south of Lille; he was to be famous a little later on.

On 27 May, AC Williamson (A/G) was killed by machine-gun

fire from one of our own fighters. Also on the 27th, Cpl Jones (A/G) was wounded and one aircraft crashed on landing. On 28th, F/O (Lt) Clapham and Sgt Brown were missing in L1720. On 31st, F/Lt Shepley and P/O Hare were missing in P9127. On the same day, P/O Biden and AC Beard went missing in L4793. A Whitley bomber tried to land; he was badly shot up and careered out of control through the perimeter fence and turned over. The men helped to rescue several of the crew. They had been dropping propaganda leaflets over Germany.

The invasion of England was now imminent. What to do with such a depleted squadron – was it RAF or was it army co-operation? It didn't seem to matter any more. They were first at Lymme aerodrome then they were moved to Redhill in Surrey for a short while. Then on to Marshal's airport in Cambridge, where they were in tents with the heavy rain sending rivulets of water among the beds. After that, they were moved to Corpus Christi College, Cambridge, for a fortnight and ate their meals with the undergraduates there.

In June Italy declared war on Britain and France, and on 13 June Mr Churchill went on his last visit to France to try to give them moral support. By 14 June, the Germans had already entered Paris; on the 18th, P/O Hayes was wounded and aircraft P1720 was destroyed on landing. On 22 June France capitulated.

One day Alfred and Lawes narrowly missed being bombed when a stray German bomber dropped a stick of bombs across Marshal's aerodrome.

The next move was to Okehampton in Devon where the men were mainly engaged on digging trenches, as great air battles were being fought above them. After a short stay there they were then moved to Western Zoyland. Were we fooling the enemy with all these moves? Or were we to be cannon fodder for an invading army?

As Alfred had now no planes to maintain he was sent on a fitter II course on engines at Gloucester; his service with 16 Squadron had ended.

There was one incident that happened at Cambridge which was still fresh in Alfred's mind when he left the squadron. On their retreat from France they escaped with only what they stood

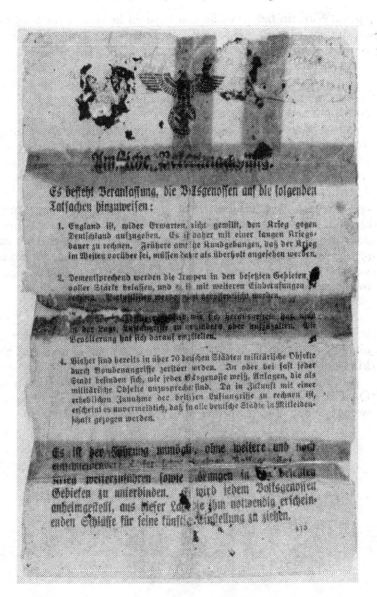

Our propaganda leaflet, recovered from a burning crash

up in. With tin hat and rifle and bayonet he went with a pal of his to the Criterion pub for a drink. There were about ten young Scottish soldiers having a drink too many. At turning-out time, when the airmen went down the adjoining passage to go to the loo, they were met by the Scottish soldiers who started shouting: 'Where were you bloody RAF blokes in France, sitting back at home while we were out there?'

It was useless trying to calm the soldiers down and explaining that their squadron had been in the thick of the battle and was still in the front line when other armies had retreated. Fists suddenly started to fly; one soldier who was wearing a ring struck Alfred above the eyebrow. It made quite a large laceration; his eyes were covered in blood. Two other soldiers knocked Lofty through the passage gates which were on a spring return. Alfred was then bundled through and the gates shut with the return spring. The airmen found themselves momentarily cut off from each other. Then up came a tipsy old hag intent on having her own private war. She commenced to knock out every pane of glass she could find with an empty beer bottle.

'Kill the bastards, kill the bastards,' she started to shout. But by this time the two airmen had escaped by jumping over a dividing wall and found themselves back in the pub yard. The MPs duly arrived and carted off the soldiers.

Around this time, in 1940, Alfred heard that his old station of Duxford was bombed by ten German bombers and six of them were shot down. One Spitfire pilot had baled out.

5

Leaving for Aden

ON 1 September Alfred obtained leave and on arrival at Derby there were air-raid warnings all night. The Germans were trying to bomb Rolls-Royce. The next day Alfred received a phone call to return to his unit at Gloucester, where he found many of his old friends from earlier days on the course, including Bob Lawes and Arthur Dunbar. The training course was intensive; some the instructors were ex-university men brought in to train the expanding personnel of the RAF.

Alfred's passing-out percentage would make him an LAC fitter IIE. (It was posted up to that effect on the notice board.) But the powers that be decided too many men had passed their LAC so three of them were demoted to fitter IIE AC First Class. Alfred was very upset as he was one of the three.

There were now thousands of Polish airmen assembled who had volunteered for the services. They looked a clean, healthy bunch of chaps.

On 9 September, the news came through that 400 people were killed and 1,460 injured after the most terrible battle over London. Raiders were over Gloucester camp on 11 September and dropped bombs without any warning – a sneak raider. The airmen dived under the workbenches for cover. On 10 September, there had been serious news of the intended invasion again. Over 200 planes had been downed over London. Twenty-five of our fighters were shot down and ten pilots escaped. Our propaganda news was again in evidence.

On 17 October 1940, all the huge naval guns surrounding the camp opened up with a terrific barrage. Several men rushed outside to dive into the air-raid shelters and found themselves in several feet of water. Those airmen who braved it out by diving under the benches were the drier ones.

Our hammer blows along the coasts of France made Hitler put off his invasion plans. Raiders were now over the camp. Many times some were chased off by our fighters, but one dropped bombs very near to us.

The Americans were now giving more aid in various ways. Germany sent troops into Romania and Russia sent troops as well. Gradually it seemed that it was developing into a great world war.

Alfred was now due for a weekend break and he boarded the train for Derby. On entering Birmingham the train was held up due to a very heavy raid over the city. As the troops sat on the blacked-out train, which was halted on the outskirts of the city, many great fires could be seen, and the terrific din of exploding shells from the AA guns.

Most of the men now passing out as fitter IIE and fitter II Airframe were men who had several years' experience in the service. They were desperately needed to go out once again to squadrons in action at home and abroad.

On 10 November 1940, Alfred's posting from Gloucester was to West Kirby where he was to be kitted out for goodness knows what or where. Obviously he was to depart from Liverpool. The train was running four hours late; on arrival the camp was a morass, the roads like rivers. Organisation was at its lowest. Nobody seemed to have a clue why they were at West Kirby and the men wanted to find out where their destination was going to be. The authorities also seemed to be unaware of this knowledge. Perhaps the intelligence service of the Germans could enlighten them.

At 10 p.m. they were called together and told to be ready at 5.30 the next morning to start the journey back to Uxbridge to be kitted out for overseas service. With the intervention of air raids they were twelve hours on the train, the 'Wailing Willies' going almost non-stop.

The *Viceroy of India*, later sunk

The men eventually found themselves at East Camp, Uxbridge. They entered the cookhouse for tea – tinned sardines – their first meal for over twelve hours. After tea there was parade for roll-call, but still they had no idea where they were destined for; everyone seemed in a flat spin; another roll-call, still nothing happening.

Eventually the men took the initiative and presented themselves at the clothing stores. The people there seemed to have some idea, for they started to almost throw overseas khaki kit at them: pith helmets, shorts, stockings, shoes and not forgetting the khaki jackets – for the use of. When Alfred's turn came and he tried the jacket for size it was all of fourteen sizes too big. He was of rather slim build, whereas the jacket had been made for some pot-bellied giant who had not yet turned up to claim it. The clothing orderly was sick and tired of the sight of it so he threw the jacket at Alfred with a look of no return on his face.

At 8 p.m. another parade and march to the dining hall to collect the unconsumed portion of the day's ration. This was to take with them on the train journey to God Knows Where.

They eventually landed up at Port Gourock at four o'clock in the morning to be loaded up on to a small ship which took them to the seaward-anchored *Viceroy of India*.

It was 16 November 1940 and the *Viceroy of India* had just been commandeered as a troop carrier. Nothing had been changed from her operating as a pleasure ship. The army and air force men were to travel as first-class passengers. She was a lovely clean ship and after the previous experience of living in tents in the atrocious English climate, and the disasters of France, Alfred felt that this was sheer luxury.

Breakfast was at 8 a.m., two eggs and bacon, porridge, bread and butter and marmalade and tea. At dinner time Alfred was beginning to feel the movement of the ship so he missed the meal. Supper time was two sausages and mashed potatoes. All the 'erks' thought they had been made up to officer status with this treatment.

On the morning of 18 November they started out to sea and were soon meeting up with other ships. Quite a few of the Strathclyde ships were sighted. It was to be one of the largest convoys that had ever sailed from the shores of Britain. On

The *Aquitainia*, in convoy

their journey they were to see the ships that had served the great British Empire. The *Aquitainia, Strathmore, Strathallen, Empress of Canada, Strathnaver, Union Castle, Warwick Castle,* the *Franconia, Arcadia, Mauretania* and others, either sailing with them or in other ports as they went around Africa to Aden and the Middle East.

These old warriors of the sea had all been gathered from around the world in the last Herculean effort to try to keep the old empire intact. The seamen serving in them committed great acts of bravery when strafed and bombed by enemy planes or torpedoed by submarines. Many of the ships and men would later lie in the depth of the oceans. But, as someone more famous once said, we will remember them.

As other large ships came into view to take up convoy positions, the warships and frigates patrolled on the perimeter. It was truly a fascinating sight to see the other ships come into view as the convoy intermittently changed course to avoid the preying submarines.

Alfred and his mates studied the stars at night more than at any time in their lives. They became quite adept at plotting the course of the ships, allowing for the change of course every now and then.

Everyone was for ever on the alert for submarines and occasionally depth charges would be dropped into the sea. Every now and then could be seen the reassuring sight of the convoy planes. The RAF personnel were mainly of non-commisioned rank, so young army officers drilled the RAF men. Some of the army drill commands differed slightly from the RAF. One young subaltern with an eye to becoming a field-marshal was drilling Alfred's squad. He called them 'Lazy good for nothings, with no drill sense, unlike the army men'.

Alfred passed the word around the men, 'On the next word of command all together bring your feet down on the deck and shake him.'

Superbly on time, all feet came down with a great thud on the deck. The subaltern did not know which way to turn, but he was cautious in his dealings with the RAF men during the rest of the month-long voyage at sea.

As it was too risky to go through the Straits of Gibraltar and the Suez Canal, the long alternative route around Africa had to be undertaken, travelling far across the oceans towards America and down through the Atlantic. Sierra Leone, on the West Coast of Africa, was the first port of call for refuelling. Further up the coast, the French at Dacca had already decided to co-operate with Hitler's Germany, so extra care was required to guard against the U-boat menace.

The convoy now rounded Africa and some of the 10,000 of the Allied troops were landed and paraded through the streets of Durban to boost the morale of South Africa. Immediately after the troops were halted and dismissed, the Australian contingent marauded through the streets of Durban. They broke all the rules of apartheid by making the African rickshaw men get into the seats of the rickshaws. The Australian soldiers then got into the shaft, pulling the smiling Africans and springing every now and then into the air mocking the motion of the beribboned-legged natives. The more war-experienced and disciplined men of the British forces looked on in subdued disbelief. They were witnessing the start of a new face of democracy.

Alfred and some of his friends were having a quiet drink in an hotel when some Australian soldiers entered the lounge and immediately picked up pints of beer belonging to some South Africans. They were not amused by the over-exuberance of the Australians. Some ships was later diverted to other ports of call.

The blazing lights of Durban were a fantastic sight to behold after total blackout in Britain and the ships at sea. As the men's journey continued, extra care was needed in the channel of Madagascar against the ever-preying submarines. Also around the Gulf of Aden for, on the opposite side, the Italians had already captured British Somaliland and, on the 13 December, Mussolini had the idea of conquering Egypt. They continued up the Red Sea and Suez Canal to finally disembark at Port Said and on to the dispersal camp at Fayid near the Western Desert.

After regrouping they were to retrace their steps back to Aden, on the old *Empress of Canada*, without any escort. She relied on

Camel Corps, near Suez Canal

her maximum boiler-bursting speed of 17 knots to try to outwit the U-boats. The *Empress of Canada* was a dirty old ship, almost at the end of her tether. The men were posted to 203 Squadron of long-standing overseas commitments; it had just turned over from Singapores, in Iraq and in Aden during the Abyssinian crisis, and was now converting to Blenheim Mark I with maximum speed of 260 mph and a bomb load of 1,000 lb. No. 203 Squadron flew reconnaissance and fighter patrols, or bomber, according to what was asked of it, mainly over the Red Sea, now that, in June 1940, Italy had entered the war. The surrounding islands in the straits around Aden were bombed in an endeavour to oust the Italians.

In the hangar at Aden stood a captured three-engined Savoia Machetti Bomber; it had landed in the desert when it ran out of fuel. The crew had been brought into camp by the natives, who no doubt were compensated for their efforts.

One of the men working out on the plain of Khormaksar airstrip developed 'Aden gut'. This bug had the ability to make one run faster than one's fastest speed in order to get to the loo on time. The said man asked his sergeant if he could be transferred to base where loos were near at hand. He was told to go and report to the sergeant there for duty. He marched into the hangar where Sergeant Selby and Alfred were working on a Blenheim. With a red perspiring face and muscles all-a-twitch, he said urgently, 'Sergeant Selby, I've come to report to you as I've got to be near a shit-house.'

Sergeant Selby coloured up with anger but then he suddenly realised what the man was desperately trying to convey when he clasped his hands to his backside and ran towards the loo. Turning to Alfred, Sergeant Selby said, 'We'd better find him a job nearer a quick exit, Alfred.'

Alfred's first meal at Aden was breakfast. He joined the queue of airmen entering the narrow passage leading between the cookhouse and dining room. A plate contained a fried egg and one rasher of bacon. Alfred held this in one hand whilst he picked up a mug of tea with the other hand, but when he turned to enter the dining room the fried egg was missing from his plate. He turned to the next man and accused him of pinching his egg. The old-lag-of-Aden said, 'You're a new sprog here aren't you? Well just watch the queue and see what happens.'

Within a few moments, swoosh, down came a kite-hawk

(otherwise known as shite-hawk to the men) and grabbed the egg from an unsuspecting sprog.

'There,' said the old lag, 'them shite-hawks know when there's a new entry of men.' Later on Alfred and his mates tried to get their own back on the kite-hawks by fastening some rinds of bacon on a long piece of string, and on the other end a rolled-up piece of paper with a length of elastic. Sure enough the kite-hawks fell for it; down swooped one with a huge wing span and grabbed the bacon in his talons; it was quite some seconds before the length of string was taken up and then, with the sudden pull on the elastic, the ball of paper shot towards the rear of the fleeing bird. It would not let go of the swirling thing behind it, but kept turning its head round and looking at this strange apparition chasing its rear. He flew further and further with other birds in hot pursuit. The airmen often wondered where he landed. One of the bright old lags soon had the answer to that, for turning to the sprogs he said, 'You've been here long enough to have seen great rings of vultures high up in the sky and that keep coming down in ever decreasing circles. Do you know where they go lads?'

Goggle-eyed the sprogs replied, 'No, where do they go?'

'Up each other's backsides,' said the old lag.

The old sweats of Aden firmly believed that the bed bugs knew when a new draft of men were about to enter camp. They maintained that the bugs all congregated in the rafter strings of the spare beds that were about to be used by the new sprogs. The more enlightened of the new draft picked up the beds and dropped them suddenly on to the floor of the barrack room. The floor was immediately covered in bugs and, on killing them by striking the floor with a shoe, the resulting smell was horrific. Tins with a drop of paraffin in were placed under the legs of the bed.

After some time in this humid camp, some men got utterly fed up, and one man went sick pretending that he had gone bonkers; on confronting the medical officer he put his outstretched hands to each side of his head and shouted, 'Boo.'

The medical officer viewed the poor man sorrowfully; then he did exactly the same thing to the man, exclaiming, 'I want to go home just as much as you, me lad.'

To relieve the boredom, Cpl Davies was showing the new draft the trick of trying to drop a rupee from off his forehead, without the use of hands, into a funnel which was stuck into the top of his shorts. He deftly bent his head downwards, and low and behold the coin slid neatly down and fell into the funnel. Abdul, an Arab cleaner, saw him do the trick and was fascinated by the thought of being able to keep the rupee. After a bit of prompting from Cpl Davies, he agreed to have a go. The funnel was placed into the top of his baggy pantaloons, the rupee was placed on his forehead. As he was busy trying to get the coin into the funnel, Cpl Davies beat him to it with a jug of water which he poured into the funnel. Abdul stood there letting the water run down inside his pantaloons until he realised he was the victim of an old Arab joke. He shouted, 'No shame, sahib, no shame.' But he did finish with several rupees to the good instead of one for being such a good sport.

The sport of the officers consisted of making up a sailblown sand-raft out of old motor car chassis and wheels. The speed attained on the broad sand below the old volcanic rocks was quite amazing. Those inclined towards the sport of fishing would sit on the exposed parts of the volcanic rocks and fish for young sharks caught in the deep pools around them.

The brilliant starlit nights opened up discussions on astronomy and, on walks along the seashore towards the old volcano, one could see birds with curved beaks similar to the curlew, pushing their beaks into the sand for small crabs. There were flocks of small brown birds with white patches round their eyes; wild ducks in profusion, including the pin-tail; storks and albatross, and buzzards who were for ever fighting. As Alfred and his mates walked back to camp, they saw two buzzards which had fought until both had broken wings and one had died; it measured five feet from wing tip to wing tip but there were others much longer than that one.

Yaks as large as buffaloes, goats and sheep with fat tails, were being driven by the Yemeni into Aden. The Yemenis had huge carved and star-studded knives strapped to their waists. One day,

Water buffalo

two of them had a trotting race with camels. Two chickos (children) played with a gazelle, teasing it until suddenly it darted towards one boy who had a long stick in his hands. He ran away but the stick got between his legs and down he went; the gazelle made good use of his horns.

When going into Aden, the taxis waited at the camp gates, charging six rupees for five men (the rupee being equal to one sixth of our money, and there were 16 annas to the rupee). In the rough homemade cafés the natives sat smoking their bubbly pipes, their four wives probably somewhere in the background.

No. 203 Squadron was now nearing the end of its role in the Abyssinian affair.

6

Back to the Desert

ON 13 April 1941, it was posted back to the Desert Campaign. The men were loaded on to an old pilgrim ship about to go on its way to the Holy Land, named the *Khosrou*. Tied to the aft rails of the ship were a number of thin, razor-backed sheep; periodically one would be unleashed and led to

Skinning sheep for pilgrims on the *Khosrou*

slaughter on the aft deck. The carcass was cut up and dumped into boilers which were heated by charcoal fires. The entrails of the sheep were thrown overboard for the sharks to feed on. The smell was terrible, and most of the men went down with stomach trouble and diarrhoea. The medical officer had thought he had pre-empted this problem by restricting the men solely to service rations, but it made not the slightest difference as every man suffered stomach trouble.

Everyone was pleased to disembark at Port Said and they were eventually taken to camp at Kabrit, landing there on 16 April 1941. A flight was dispatched to Heraklion in Crete.

Alfred had read a book about Kitchener in Egypt when he became sirdar (commander-in-chief) during the battle of Tel-el-Kebir against Egypt and had noticed the date of 13 September 1882. How many times, he wondered, would the number 13 crop up during this present conflict?

On 27 April 1941, there was an engagement involving 8 Blenheims, approximately 20 JU87s, 8 ME 110s, and an unknown number of ME 109s were sighted. Aircraft L9237 and her crew was feared lost (F/Lt Whittal may have been the pilot). The squadron was operating in the Western Desert and also at Heraklion in Crete at this time. Part of it was now facing the Great Bitter Lake and the khamsin winds blowing across the eastern desert made life equivalent to being in an oven, sending the temperature to around 110 degrees. And one had to walk nearly a quarter of a mile for the sea to be deep enough to swim.

Planes with great circular metal rings around them constantly flew overhead and on to the Gulf of Suez in the endeavour to set off enemy mines. It was as well to be as far away as possible on these occasions. But they were not to stay here much longer – 203 Squadron began to get updated with Mark IV Blenheims.

In February 1941 the Australians had captured Tobruk, but in April Rommel advanced and closed round it. The 8th Army fell back to Sidi-Rezegh. Part of 203 Squadron was loaded on to a desert train to take it back to the eastern side of the Suez, to Quassassin, to guard against the uprising of King Farouk against the British. As the train was travelling over the British-built desert railway, some Arabs had somehow or other boarded the train in an attempt to steal the airmen's equipment. They had overpowered an armed guard, but a hefty British airman called Blatherwick, from Nottingham, was not to be intimidated. He grabbed the rifle, which the Arab had stolen and then picking up the Arab by the scruff of the neck and the seat of his pantaloons, he threw him bodily from the train.

Tired and fed up, they eventually arrived, but they had been stoned on the journey by some Egyptian boys. On the camp someone had rigged up five showers; these consisted of five petrol tins with perforated bottoms and slung high upon a crossbar and fed with one supply pipe, the enclosure being surrounded by sacking. Lying on the floor was a slightly inebriated airman, still with his clothes on, being soaked by the dripping water. He murmured, 'You are good chaps to me, for looking after me like this.' Needless to say, the older sprogs were not taking the slightest interest in his welfare for they were carrying on with their luxurious ablution.

A day later a lorry load of men were allowed to go swimming. They were on an elevated sand bank near the sea. Instead of walking into the sea until it was deep enough to swim in, one of the men decided to dive in off the sand bank, not realising how shallow the water was at that point. This was in full view of King Farouk's luxury ship. The man's head struck the bottom of the water, and resulted in a broken neck. Two chaps hauled him out. The poor man must have realised his inevitable fate for he asked one of them to write to his invalid mother and to his girl in South Africa. He died the same night. Apparently he was the sole breadwinner of the family, for his father was dead and his only brother was paralysed. One wonders why such a tragedy should be cast upon this unlucky family. He was 203 Squadron's first ground personnel casualty in Egypt.

The entry in Official Records read: 'Signal received from Headquarters. Iraq reported aircraft T 2072 (Flying Officer Gordon Hall, Sergeant Poole and Sergeant Oultram) as missing on operations'.

On Alfred's day off, he was just a solitary being in a cluster of tents, the only noises those of high powered aero-engines running up prior to take off. But no – it was the buzzing sound of myriads of insects all intent on consuming his body. Mosquitoes in his hair, on his face, arms and body. On the following night, Alfred was guard commander; as he sat in the Guardroom Marquee,

Corporal Alfred Barker, after the first retreat

with both flaps open, the mosquitoes flew in like bombing planes coming in for refill. He was covered in stinging, itching pain, reminding him of nettle stings.

Early morning and Alfred watched the sun rising. Beyond the tent was a ridge of sand, in the foreground camel-scrub and a few small bush plants. Just before the sun appeared over the ridge, there was a deep red glow on the horizon, extending the full width of the ridge. Fascinated, Alfred tried to determine the exact spot of the sun's first appearance. All at once the beginning of a huge red ball, glowing ever more as it grew in size, raised its brilliant head above the horizon; its movement appeared to increase, until suddenly it seemed to free itself of earthly sand and appeared suspended in mid-air. Moving gradually on its way to make a great arc across the earth, heating the desert sands as its strength grew, until the temperature was 100° to 120°. When the all-powerful sun had reached over two feet of its arc, Alfred knew that his guard duty was near its end.

As surely as the sun rises, so each day saw the monotonous grind of the men, as they endeavoured to keep planes serviceable in blinding heat or blinding sandstorms. Covered in pestering flies that had probably been feeding on dead bodies, and breathing in suffocating dust stirred up by manoeuvring tanks and lorries, they did not know where that day, and the next, were going to lead them, except that they hoped it would one day be nearer the end of the war.

The rolling centuries of Egypt could not care less: she had witnessed many wars come and go over the thousands of years, her historical monuments in the form of the Pyramids standing as sentinels in proof of her old age. The benign features of the great Sphinx, made slightly more grotesque with part of its nose missing, attributed to earlier days of Napoleon's reign, still gazed down unperturbed on to the desert scene.

The base camp was now near Berg-el-Arab for 203 Squadron; it was some forty miles up the desert road known as Landing Ground (LG) 101. The Blenheims were operated from there on bombing, fighting, air sea rescue, shipping lane patrols and any other duty demanded of the squadron, A, B and C

A Blenheim crash in Aden

Flights taking it in turns to the requirements of other theatres of war.

On 10 May 1941 Aircraft L9174 was lost with her crew in the desert south of Rutbah fort. The crew were: Squadron Leader Percy Gethin who was rescued, but died at base; Sergeant Cruttenden and Sergeant White, who were both killed instantly.

General Wavell was in charge of the Desert Rats, of which there were two divisions in the Western Desert: the 7th Armoured Division stationed in the southern line, and the 4th Indian Division in the centre, with Australian and South African battalions on the northern bridgehead.

In June 1941, Auchinleck took over the Middle East command from Wavell, who then was sent to India. In the seesaw of battles, our waltzing-Matilda tanks were no match for the better gunned German tanks, and their anti-aircraft guns, which they used to such good effect against our tanks. Mail from home to the men out there almost ceased during one period, and the men talked of boarding ships at Aden with a view to carrying on the war from America. The records of the service men had not yet come through from England, which delayed promotion. Alfred was an aircraft engine fitter and worked in the maintenance section of 203 Squadron, until moved to one of the flights in later days.

A, B and C Flights operated individually as far as the uprising in Persia (Iraq), Iran, Cyprus and the Greek Islands. Around this time the Iraqi revolutionaries had besieged the British air base at Habanya. No. 203 Squadron was called upon to intervene.

On 19 August 1941, a Blenheim crashed into the sea. Two crew members, Sergeant Boothe and Crossley were rescued: the third, P/O Smith (navigator) was lost when the aircraft broke in half and sank. Casualties were now on the increase in 203 Squadron.

One of 203 Squadron's flights was caught up in the German advance into Greece. The planes were being checked by the fitters and riggers when suddenly they had to make a quick getaway. The planes' engine nacelle cowlings were left on the runway. The King of Greece was evacuated.

Engine changes in the desert were done by wheeling the aircraft under the wooden overhead gantry. The engine was then disconnected and hauled upwards by hand-operated chain pulley. The plane was then pushed backward to allow the old engine to be lowered and the new, or reconditioned, engine hauled upwards, the plane then pushed back under the gantry and the engine fitted. A truly slow procedure in times of war, our more modern mobile cranes being in short supply. This was another example of our leaders with First World War mentality.

The maintenance of aircraft was extremely difficult in this wilderness of sand, where there were no trees, hedges, grass or buildings to steady the onslaught of sandstorms. As far as the eye could see, desert sands, easily whipped up into blinding sandstorms: sand in your eyes, up your nose, in your ears; thickening in density until vision was nil. Many were the times when the men retracing their steps from the Maintenance Section back to base had to follow the telephone cable by picking it up from the sand and following it back to base.

Planes were in very short supply in the early days of the war,

Hartel, Remnant and Alfred (right) at Berg-el-Arab

particularly in the threatened Middle and Far Eastern countries. Our shipping, loaded with spare engines and equipment, was being sunk, and some of the older bi-planes were no match for the German fighters. The meals were cooked on a captured German field kitchen, the source of heating being waste oil dripping into the fireplace from one side and water dripping into the fireplace on the other side; this broke up the oil into a spluttering ringlet of flames.

The only relief from the blazing sun was the shade of the tents, but that shade also attracted scorpions, lizards, snakes, fleas, ants and other insects. But this desert scene was to be 203 Squadron's home for nigh on three years, advancing and retreating as the armies went back and forth.

On 10 October 1941, Aircraft L is officially recorded as disappearing while on the Northern Track of Crete-Libyan patrols. The crew were: P/O Rowntree, Sergeant Edwards and Sergeant Norton. The squadron flight was operating from Heraklion during this period.

Alfred wrote the following letter to his Uncle John at Smerrels Farm on the ancient Chandos Pole Estate:

I am writing this letter as I sit on my bed made out of empty petrol tins now filled with sand, my locker is also of petrol tins [these were squarish thin tins of around 8 square inches by 12 deep].

For light I have a hurricane lamp and a small lamp which I bought for eight piastres (1s. 8d.) In an old beer jug I have a few wild flowers which grow sparsely amongst the rocky areas, I think they are anemones. The only other article is a small mirror in anticipation of a shave should we get enough water. But now times are changing in this respect for it is now winter season, we have changed clothing from the RAF khaki shirt and shorts to army uniform.

It is pelting it down with rain and a strong wind is driving through here and there in the tent. This is about the fifth period of rain we've had this winter which lasts for two

The Spinx and Pyramid

or three days at a time, then it clears up and no more for weeks and weeks.

When it gets rough we are constantly aroused out of beds to peg the tent down again. There's precious little vegetation, only a little camel scrub, this great plain is relieved only here and there by rocky hills and sand dunes. The summer months are so hot it is better to work in the early morning and in the evening, but of course the war interferes with that idea.

The perspiration stands out in beads, this attracts the myriads of flies which for ever crawl into your eyes, ears and nose. When working on aircraft, holding something with your left hand and a spanner in your right hand, you let fly at the pests, they fly off unhurt but you end up with a lump where you hit yourself with the spanner.

One's nerves become frayed for, after the plague of flies there is the inevitable sandstorm, which very often causes gippo-gut, when you have to run faster than your legs can carry you to the tin bucket

A scorpion

Some of the men for entertainment will make a ring of petrol in the desert and drop a scorpion in the centre. Then they drop in a huge spider with four jaws rather like four beaks of a bird which close inwards. The ring of petrol is then ignited and the trapped victims try to kill each other. Very often the spider wins the battle by cutting off the deadly sting of the scorpion as he raises his tail to strike. The spider is then given his freedom.

It would appear that cruelty is inherent in most human beings. The Bedouin women are for ever busy with their eyes covered with their yashmak and their black and yellow robes. The patriarchal male wearing his keffiyeh head-dress and baggy pantaloons for ever kneeling towards the east; for they are devout believers. The children (chicos) usually have a huge ring in one of their nostrils, while the boys have one large ring hanging from either ear; the weight of which will wear down the flesh to the extremity of the ear lobe. The tethered buffalo with ears almost dropping off where their tethering ring has worn the ear right through. The oxen passing weary day to weary day, traversing his never-ending circular journey round the confines of the water hole, pushing the wooden arm of the ancient water wheel. Their eyes covered with sacking, veiled like the Bedouin women. Oxen and donkeys are used for ploughing the uncertain, some fertile bits of desert [this was mainly describing the Delta area].

On 9 October 1941, the Official Record reads: 'On this day's patrol aircraft K (F/O Screeton, F/O Tweedie and Sergeant Holbrook) did not return from patrol on the Northern Track.'

Back at base camp one day, Alfred noticed a cloud of dust arising in the distance. He shouted to his mate Bill Groom: 'Come over here, Bill, and look at this lot coming towards us.' They were always wary of convoys in the distance, but this could not be enemy as it was approaching from a friendly position. As the column drew nearer, their attention was drawn to the upstanding gantry of a coles-crane standing up proud above the

A native woman

A water wheel

other vehicles and displaying a hanging sign – 'Up the Derby Rams'. As Alfred was a Derby man, he felt proud to see his local football team in loud unmistakable letters displayed in the midst of the Great Western Desert.

On 13 October 1941, it was recorded that Aircraft M was missing on the Northern Track of Crete-Libyan patrols. The crew were: F/O Washington, Sergeant Young and Sergeant Bremner. It would appear that 203 Squadron Northern Track was a disastrous area. The loss of men and planes was beginning to take its toll.

Rations now began to be in short supply, bully beef was the staple diet, fried, baked, boiled and then any remains made into soup. Some bright spark in remote authority thought up the bright idea of providing a little relief in the diet, in the way of greens. He introduced dried boiled cabbage; a few handfuls, chucked into the boiling water of the field kitchen, had amazing results. It swelled up above the rim of the boiler and with the strength of a ten-ton bomb it spread its deadly smell far and wide. No one could face it, or its companion of bully beef, and it was immediately discontinued.

Our new Matilda tanks were still no match against the huge anti-tank guns of the Germans. Alfred had noticed that when the Germans had to suddenly retreat and leave their anti-tank guns behind, they blew out the end of the nozzle. The huge, skyward-pointing nozzles resembled elephants' trunks split asunder whilst raised in anger.

Auchinleck being now in charge, he was fortunate to see new supplies coming in which mainly Wavell had been denied. Rommel now proposed to attack Tobruk. Sir Alan Cunningham was in charge of the Commonwealth troops.

The 8th Army were named as 13 and 30 Corps. The NZ engineers extended the one railway line up the desert, while the Australians were relieved and replaced by the British and Polish troops. An attempt was made to capture Rommel at Athens but he was away at the time. Men of 203 Squadron brought back the news when their flight returned to base. Nos. 13 and 30 Corps had been in the thick of the fighting and Rommel ordered their destruction. But an order and its execution were two different things. The Italians and Germans were now back around Mersa Brega. The 203 Squadron was busy sub spotting, escort duty or bombing. Many ships, including the *Ark Royal*, were sunk.

Water was scarce, every drop for a full squadron of men had to be carted by water bowser. One man from each tent took it in turns to collect about half a gallon by signing for it for their particular tent. It had to suffice for drinking and washing for around five men until the following day's supply. Rumour had it that the Germans sometimes contaminated the water of the oasis, and often brackish water had to be used. Rations became very scarce indeed, for other theatres of war drew on the ever-decreasing supplies as our ships were constantly the target of enemy bombers and submarines. Tank crews had to have sufficient food supplies with them, but who could envy them? Trapped in the confines of an overheated tank was worse than dreadful.

The RAF squadrons, dotted here and there in the desert areas, had to survive for periods on a shoe-string. Many of the planes were kept flying on the ingenuity of the ground crews. Around this period the men started to discuss with each other the phenomenon of having hallucinating dreams. Alfred told Paddy Bonner about the vivid recurring dream he had of seeing Derby Cathedral vividly outlined in the middle of a circle of white cloud, the four corners of the spires high above the cloud. The dream occurred night after night as if trying to convey some hidden message. Other times he would have vivid dreams of his parents' farmhouse, with only his mother alive in it and the rain pouring through a dilapidated roof, while the hymn was being sung by an unseen choir: 'Change and decay in all around I see, In life, in death, Oh Lord abide with me.' Another man spoke of his recurring dreams, which came in chapters, like reading a book. The next morning he would recount the continuing saga. All the men agreed on one thing and that was the overriding vividness of the dreams.

The German Junkers 87 and Stuka dive bombers were now very active.

On 25 November 1941, the entry in Official Records read, 'A Wellington of the Sea-Rescue Flight, which had searched for and sighted a dinghy in position 32°14'N, 25°51'E, crashed on landing at base, and immediately caught fire. One only out of a crew of six was saved.' It was a sad reflection that those in the dinghy were saved at the price of the lives who helped to save them.

A Commander Luigi de la Penne led three two-men midget submarines into Alexandria Harbour and sank HMS *Valiant* and then stuck a depth charge on the *Queen Elizabeth*. No. 203 Squadron's men on their one-day-a-month visit to Alexandria brought back the sad news to the squadron. Everything seemed to be against us at this particular stage of world affairs. But better news came – America had now entered the war, for on 19 December Churchill had been to see the US President Roosevelt. This was soon followed by bad news, however. For, on that day, it was recorded that Aircraft E (F/O Read, Sgt Brown, Sgt McLevy) failed to return. Tubby, the squadron blacksmith, was a big fine young man and very adept with his blow lamp and

203 Squadron captured this Stuka dive bomber at Bengazi

welding kit. He could knock anything together for the use of the squadron and it was amazing the number of things that he was asked to make out of the 40-gallon petrol drums. Tubby was about to set to work on an empty drum that had stood in the hot sun with all the caps removed to evaporate any fumes that may have been in the barrel. When he applied the welder with a view to cutting a piece out of the barrel, a mighty explosion occurred; the 40-gallon drum and poor Tubby were blown to kingdom come. He was sadly missed by the men.

A new warrant officer of general duties now arrived on the squadron. The older-type sprogs of the desert were fit, lithe, suntanned men. Warrant Officer Ward stood out like a sore thumb with his long shorts half covering his fat knees, his forearms only just protruding through the sleeves of his khaki shirt. Two fat hands, apparently stuck on to his wrist as an afterthought, were gesticulating wildly in an endeavour to attract the Boss Rice, who was an Arab Chief of the ten Arab underlings. Boss Rice was waving his *kourbash* (whip) threateningly at his underlings, but never actually touching them with it. It was all a posture to prove that they could be more adequate than the British in organising labour. As the Arabs and their mighty Boss Rice stood awaiting orders from the new English Boss Ward, he was at a quandary for the lack of knowledge of Arabic words. He turned to a desert-weary corporal and said, 'What do I say in Arabic for "Come here, do this?"'

'Oh, just shout to them: *Saida iggri – yalla imshi, yimkin bardi bukra.*' This meant in rough Arabic: 'Hello, sod off till day after tomorrow' which of course they immediately started to do. Warrant Officer Ward stood there nonplussed. The desert-weary corporal had to retrieve the situation by shouting: '*Tala hinna, mahleesh ackers*' which meant 'Come here, or you'll get no money'.

One man back at base camp decided that to relieve them of the boredom of desert life some form of entertainment was required. Bill Groom formed an entertainment committee which organised darts matches and mock football, to bring in those men who normally did not play football. As it was nearing Christmas, they were intent on organising a Christmas Party, irrespective of whether they were in the position of advance or retreat. Old tentage and cast-off parts of aircraft were used for this purpose. It was quite amazing, the ingenuity of the men, when we saw the finished product. Alfred and other members of the committee worked as the mock bar in their odd hours off from duty. Crates of beer were diligently saved from the ration of the non-drinkers. The officers provided odd bottles of whisky which were normally denied the men. Everyone scrounged and saved for the coming party at base camp, which was still at landing ground 101. The cooks did a wonderful job of providing luxuries out of thin air. A wonderful Christmas party was the final result.

Thereafter Alfred was to be the main organiser of the welfare on the squadron. The strange phenomenon of number 13's appearance yet again reared its head when Bill Groom informed Alfred that he was the twelfth child of a family of 13.

The beleaguered Island of Malta was now in dire need of

supplies, for the ships of supply were the constant targets of the German and Italian planes and submarines. No. 203 Squadron was called to escort the ships towards Malta with their Mark IV Blenheims. If the crews exceeded the planes' limits of distance then they were forced to ditch into the sea.

On 23 January 1942, records state that at 13.06 a message was picked up from aircraft M: WJRS OS 13.07 message 'Am landing in the sea'. The estimated position of this aircraft was 34°00'N 21°45'E. The other Blenheim on patrol carried out a search in this area but failed to see anything. At 14.25 one Maryland was airborne on Just 7 to carry out a search over that part of the patrol where it was estimated that Blenheim M had force-landed. This aircraft returned at 18.45 with nil report. The crew of Blenheim M were F/Lt Green, Sgt Giles and F/Sgt Dawson DFM.

Around this time, 203 Squadron was operating at Berka 3 near Bengazi and a captured Stuka dive bomber was brought back to base, which boosted the morale of the men considerably.

The operations flight at Gambut were issued with Marylands, with twin Wasp engines and having a good turn of speed. They were ideal for photographic reconnaissance, with a speed of 278 mph. Times were beginning to change from the days when at one critical period there was only one serviceable aircraft of Blenheims on the squadron. Spares at that time were not getting through and when reconditioned ones did get delivered their serviceable life was only a fraction of what it should have been. Unserviceable planes had to be robbed to try to keep others serviceable. Alfred had to make a tommy bar out of a half shaft of a lorry to operate the spanner for releasing the retaining nut on the airscrews. Wing Commander Johnson, a tall man of vibrant personality, in his short stay with 203 Squadron, realised that there seemed to be a dire need to shake up those sand-happy desert rats. He could not comprehend why so many of the squadron planes were unserviceable, and all at the same time.

The week prior to his arrival there had been several air casualties and some of the worst sandstorms in the desert, and work on planes was brought to a standstill. Turning to the young

A Wellington crash at Berg-el-Arab, 1942

fed-up mechanic he barked, 'My man, why is my plane not serviceable to fly?'

The reply was quick and to the point: 'Because, sir, you forgot to order the cease-fire of the sandstorms.' The technical sergeant, secretly grinning to himself, quickly intervened and explained the difficulties of exposing engine parts to the onslaught of the uncontrollable weather. Feeling a short, very temporary, sense of guilt, the commander thought he would make a further inspection of the maintenance section, way out in the blue. Here the men worked in blazing sun up to 120° or more, or in blinding sandstorms, in a vain effort to keep the planes serviceable.

There were no canteen facilities and no arrangements to even make a cup of tea. C/O Johnson quickly altered that; he organised a supply of tea, milk and sugar and left the maintenance men to fix up a primus stove, on top of which they precariously balanced a gallon-petrol tin full of water. Sometime later Wing Commander Johnson reappeared and saw the queue of airmen with mugs at the ready. He marched to the front of the queue, tapped the tea maker on the shoulder and was about to ask him how things were going. Without looking round the sprog shouted: 'Get behind the fucking queue, you silly bugger, I can't serve two bloody people at the same time, can I?'

He then turned and saw that it was the Commanding Officer. It was credit due that Wing Commander Johnson's sense of humour came to the fore, and he and the men shared in the joke with ribald laughter.

Corporal Bond, Alfred's tried and trusted friend, lived in the same tent with three other airmen. He abhorred the sight of scorpions, especially the black variety which were said to be much more dangerous than the yellow ones. As he took off his one garment of clothing, which was an overall and jacket combined, he hung it up on a nail which had been driven into the tent pole. 'There!' said he, 'the buggers won't get into it there.' The next morning he donned the garment, suddenly let out a cry and jumped out of the overalls. A black scorpion went scurrying out of the tent. Corporal Bond had been stung in the middle of his back. He was rushed to the medical tent and was injected with serum. He was to live successfully through that episode, only to face a far greater tragedy later in the story.

In the early days of the Desert War, there was precious little contact between the men and their commanders as the battles went back and forth. One did not seem to know where they would be from one day to the next. In the early days of the war, Gladiator bi-planes, early type Rolls-Royce armoured cars and early Blenheims were used; it was also fortunate that many of the Italian planes were of the early type bi-planes. The four-engined Handley Page Hampton with a speed of 265 mph was now in service over here.

Water was getting ever scarcer; the Bedouins were now search- ing deeper and deeper for water in the *wadi*. Corporal Bond said to Alfred, 'Let's go over and look at what they're up to.'

Some Arab women and young girls were there with donkeys;

The flight of 203 Squadron on Blenheims in the Western Desert

Corporal Bond, later killed in an air crash, tries his hand at ploughing

each one carried a couple of the empty RAF cast-off petrol tins, others carried goatskin containers. As the two men gazed down the shaft of the well they could see big boulders with a narrow jetty running along the bottom and disappearing into the bowels of the earth. An Arab chico was seen crawling along under the ledge, returning later with a full petrol tin of water. Further up the valley the only other well was completely dry. There, the meagre crop of wheat had completely perished, one or two dried shoots being the only proof that anything had ever grown there. The two men thought of the words – 'and there was famine in Egypt'. The only plant that had survived was the Anzel plant. As ever, the chicos came and asked for *baksheeh* (money). They had their eyes almost closed with the discharge from some eye disease. Their lucky, but dirty, goats-foot talisman hung around their necks, but this was letting them down on charms right now. To show off before the eyes of the Engleesi they both started to throw stones by means of a sling, much as David had done thousands of years before. Quite a bond of camaraderie was developing between the Commonwealth troops and the Bedouin tribesmen.

A little further on the scarab beetle was busy with his armour-plated body and universal jointed legs. He was feeling his way with his vertebrae round a ball of food, more than twice his own size. He turned and with his two back legs pushed it backwards, his front and centre legs taking the strain; every now and then he would cease pushing and would traverse the ball of food to ascertain that it was going in the right direction to the hole that he had dug. Eventually, with much manoeuvring, he eventually pushed the ball of food into the hole some yards away and covered it with sand. Many times during the long period in the desert, the men would watch these gargantuan feats of the sacred scarab beetle. The bird life seemed to have disappeared again, but on odd occasions starlings, lapwings and native birds could be seen. But the little wagtail still strutted around.

The squadron now began to be issued with one or two Hudson aircraft and were operating from LG 39 and LGY. On 6 April 1942, it was recorded that between 02.25 and 03.25, LG 05 (landing ground 235 Wing) was attacked by 5 twin-engined bombers; about 10 bombs were dropped, 3,250 KG bombs falling near the landing ground. The bombs were shallow dive attacks carried out from low level. One of those bombs was a direct hit on the Operations Room. Two officers and three other ranks were killed, one of the officers being S/Ldr Scott, who was controller on duty at the time. S/Ldr Scott had been with 203 Squadron since its early days at Aden and was Flight Commander until the beginning of the year, when he left to take Control Duties at 235 Wing.

As the build-up got underway, an Australian squadron of Baltimores settled down in the desert near to 203 Squadron. The chaps were new to desert life and the way of the Bedouin Arabs, whereas we were using the Bedouins as supernumerary guards around the outskirts of the dispersal planes in the desert. They had proved useful in preventing raiding Arabs from stealing petrol barrels, parachutes or anything they could lay their hands on. One night, the raiding Arabs had been particularly successful in stealing the full drums of petrol by approaching the camp by camel on the other side of a sand ridge. They then lay down head to foot in the desert sands and rolled the barrels from one man to the other, back to the waiting camels. The Bedouin guards had sounded the alarm and our guards started to fire their rifles. Pandemonium was let loose with rifle shots whizzing here, there and everywhere.

Alfred bore the nickname Cpl 'Colonel' Barker after someone had remembered the story of the lady who had served as a male officer some years earlier. He was guard commander in the dispersal point, when there was a sudden arrival of two very irate Australians, one an officer and one a corporal. They were brandishing their revolvers and threatened to shoot any Arab they came across. The officer spied Alfred's supernumerary Bedouin guard and Alfred had to be quick to intervene and explain the difference between town and village marauders and the trusted Bedouins. The officer said that they had been invaded by the village Arabs and one had shot one of his guards. Alfred pointed out to the officer that the intelligence service of the Arabs was renowned in knowing when a new squadron came to the desert, and ripe for the pickings.

No. 203 Squadron was to be the custodian and caretaker of this Australian Squadron for a short while. Their personnel were to feed in the mess tents of 203 Squadron and draw on the rations. The overlong queues of British and Australian men caused ill feelings. Suddenly fists began to fly, the big strong Aussies were downing our men like ninepins until, realising there was a fight on, the leaner, fit, desert Pommies and particularly the Irish, started a counter-offensive. The Aussies were now being downed quicker than the Pommies. As each body fell on to the desert sand so did a more enlightened feeling pass between the contestants. The more or less equalisation of fisticuffs started up a firm comradeship between the men. Eventually, when the Aussies organised their own Messing arrangements, they invited the Pommies to a party. Thereafter they were as one, turning their efforts into combating the increasing activity of the enemy.

The worn-out old piano with several notes stuck down with the spillings of beer matched the desert-happy man sitting on its stool. Sam repeatedly churned out a repetitious, one-handed tune as he half-turned towards the men, and half-turned to the piano. Menacingly, he held aloft a beer bottle in his left hand, ready to down anyone who should have the audacity to object to his repeated melody. But Sam's mental stability was deteriorating and one night he was observed wandering around the camp in his night-shirt. Having been plied with stale beer by ulterior-motived men to get him off the piano, he paused at the tent of the commanding officer. As he stood in the doorway of Wing Commander Johnson's tent he kept shouting, 'I've come for him, I've come for him.'

'Who have you come for?' said the weary-eyed C/O. 'The Holy Ghost,' replied Sam.

The following day he was visited by the Holy Ghost in the form of the new medical officer, aptly named Bloomer. Now Bloomer was also an outstanding creature. He was an Australian bush doctor. He wore long shorts, wrinkled stockings, large brown boots and his squat figure was topped by an over-sized Australian hat, which made his squat figure shorter than ever. The men called him the 'vet', for rumour would have it that an unfortunate man, who had gangrene in his big toe, had it sliced off by Bloomer when he was told to 'look the other way'.

Although his methods were somewhat vet-like they were effective in this land of medical shortages. Bloomer got Sam an early return to England and the land of better pianos.

A lone German bomber one night found his free passage down the valley and, on finding 203 Squadron undefended, he dropped a stick of bombs across the maintenance section tents. When Technical Officer Martin rushed out of the tent and into the moonlight, he saw what he thought was a trench. But moonlight can play dirty tricks on a petrified man in the desert. Technical Officer Martin took a mighty leap to dive into the trench, but he landed face down in a shadow on the desert sands. The resulting bruises on his face prevented him hiding his misfortune. An airman named Pigge, needless to say a comedian called The Pig, was always on the lookout for ribald material for his concert jokes. This little episode was added to his future entertainment on the squadron.

A plane force-landed on the edge of the Quattara Depression. Alfred and two other airmen were sent to investigate the cause of the landing and the salvage of the Baltimore aircraft, with long-range fuel tanks fitted. A fuel box for selecting fuel from one tank to another was fitted. The selector cock was turned and with a click it dropped into the on position, but the pilot had not turned the cock sufficiently, thus it was riding half-way between the position from one tank to another and had starved the motors of fuel. Alfred felt that the extra addition of a small red dot to mark the positions would have probably prevented this forced landing. The aircraft was later flown safely back to base. Many modifications of aircraft were often the result of these investigations when passed on to higher authority. The Quattara Depression was made up of a vast wasteland of soft marsh and sand and undermined by salt water. The blazing sun turning vast areas into salt, feet thick and, in other places, very thin layers which would give way to a man's weight. A place to be avoided by the tanks, troops and planes.

Official records for 14 April 1942 state, firstly, that F/Lt Bowker, Sgt Hayes and Sgt Parsons set off from LG 05 at 09.40 hrs on a special search to the south-west of Crete. No signal was received from the aircraft and it failed to return to base. Nothing has since been heard of the fate of this crew which had only recently started operating with this squadron. Secondly, at about 07.00 hrs P/O Halbert, F/O Somerville, F/Sgt Gordon and Sgt Rogers set off from LG 05 on an extended reconnaissance for enemy shipping on the south-west and west of Crete. At 10.00 hrs this crew sighted 2 M/Us, 1 cruiser and 5 destroyers, co.190°, speed 10 knots, in position 36°35'N 16°42'E. At 10.15 hrs, in position 36°48'N 16°42'E, 2 destroyers were reported on co.010°, speed 15 knots. A later signal sent at 10.55 hrs reported 4 M/Vs (4,000–6,000 tons) and 5 destroyers, on a course of 200° and travelling at 8 knots in position 36°24'N 16°35'E ... The enemy forces were shadowed by this aircraft for two and a half hours and a decision was made by the crew to land at Malta in full daylight. Probably as a result of the signals sent by Maryland Z, the Germans had sent a strong fighter force over Malta. After their last signal at 12.30 hrs nothing more was heard of them and they failed to arrive at Malta (A/C Maryland 298).

Much is to be said for the bravery of the air crews on these hazardous missions.

The order went up on the noticeboard for volunteer NCOs required for dangerous duties with the resistance movement to be parachuted into Yugoslavia. Feeling the urge for a more positive approach to the enemy, Alfred applied, but his application was turned down; he was to stay with 203 Squadron for a much longer period.

Churchill decided to send some divisions to the Far East; this resulted in retarding Auchinleck's advance. Events were proving that all the outposts of the great empire could not adequately be defended at one and the same time.

Our men's only resemblance to having a bath was to travel across the desert road, to bathe in the turbulent sea. A pick-up vehicle, used mainly for conveying air crews to the planes, was used on this particular day to convey a tightly packed number of air crew on the open rear of the vehicle to go for a swim, the driver and his mate being in the closed-in part of the vehicle. Whilst swimming, the swimmers got mixed up with several Italian bodies and a small mine. The men had all been warned on squadron noticeboards 'not to pick up any object that lay around for fear of booby traps' left by the enemy.

The orders were completely ignored on this occasion, for the Armament Technical Officer, who was with the swimmers, investigated the mine, and he was sure that he had made it safe. He had the audacity to load it on to the vehicle to further investigate back at camp, to find out how it worked. He was very soon to discover this. The rest of the air crew filed themselves on to the open rear of the pick-up truck and started their journey back to camp. As they turned off the road to travel over the desert sands towards base, they were almost entering the compound when they went over a sand dune. The mine exploded and the tight-knit bodies took the brunt of the explosion. They were all killed, except the driver and his mate in the closed-in part of the vehicle.

The first man on the scene was the Arab *dobie wallah* who, out of breath after running to the scene of mutilated bodies, had a heart attack and died. A further notice went upon the noticeboard warning yet again the dangers of picking up strange objects.*

To add one sad incident to another is to note the fact that some of the replacement air crews from Britain had venereal disease.

In a letter for home Alfred describes the conditions in the desert:

> The wind started to rise and blow straight through on to the flaps of the tent, they blew inwards, when the resulting wind current blew outwards again, each pressure overcoming the other in turn. At 6.30 p.m. the storms intensified, one of the chaps started to hunt for tent pegs for his side of the tent was blowing outwards. Four of the other men, during the night, were kept busy with securing tent pegs. On Saturday night at 6.30 the storm abated, it had been more or less constant for three days.

* In later years, I found no reference to this incident in the records of the squadron.

A desert storm brewing

All the men were utterly fed up with it, for the sand made their eyes sore, the dust sticks to moist lips and eventually finds its way into one's mouth, until one's teeth are like grindstones.

Every Saturday morning for the last six weeks there has been a sand storm. Now on Sunday morning it is fine, all the men's spirits are rising again. But work on the aircraft has trebled in the meantime.

Monday morning turned out beautiful, but at about ten in the morning the westerly wind sprang up again and by 11 a.m. it had developed into the worst storm we have ever had.

The men had to retreat to their tents again, and had difficulty in finding them through the murky haze of sand and dust.

The larger pebbles of sand were making a noise on the tent like hailstones. The tent next door has disappeared, the poles of another were broken, leaving the occupants to the mercy of the elements. Every few minutes one could hear the shouts of 'I'm lost, where's my tent?' The cooks could not work, for their marquee had disappeared. Tins of bully beef dug out of the sand were sliced and put on bread and sand to eat. At 3.30 p.m. the storm abated, it was then one noticed how difficult it was to breathe, with all the dirt in one's lungs.

Hoping this letter finds you well.

One got so used to one's squadron section of the desert that any outside news was often embroidered a little. Some of the chaps said they had seen Hurricanes but then others thought it a joke. But for some time, in fact, Hurricanes and Tomahawks and Kittyhawks had been sent to modernise and build up the RAF but still the 109 Messerschmitt could outwit them.

A good bit of news filtered through to Alfred that a sergeant air gunner, who had been with him in the early days of France, had been awarded the DFM for devotion to duty in shooting down an ME 110.

The men's spirits were often kept up by the actions of the enemy in broadcasting the sexy voice in the song of 'Lilli Marlene'.

Rommel had now attacked Agedalia; our line of communication was causing problems with his supplies as it had done towards the enemy in earlier days. And so the seesaw of battles went on and on.

One day, Corporal Bond and Corporal (Colonel) Barker took a short walk to investigate some tented Bedouins. They noticed that they had attempted to grow a small patch of wheat, but the desert Anzel plant was creeping in, covering the light crop. These desert dwellers must be the world's greatest optimists. An Arab man and chico came up to the two men from where they had been tending a few goats. A bony donkey stood dejectedly hobbled by his two forefeet. The poor thing could not have gone far without the hobbles, for his bones were sticking out in all directions. The hoofs of his feet were overgrown and curled upwards.

The Arabs greeted the two airmen with *saida*, and they replied

Corporal Barker viewing the area of El-Alamein before the battles

with *saida ez zajak.* The Arab father then produced a sheet of paper, rather grubby looking. He proffered it to the two airman. They read, 'This native supplies very good boiled eggs, and is recommended by me, signed Sgt Rhodes.' He had acquired it from the nearby army camp. On past experience Cpl Bond and Col Barker recalled the day when they thought they were on a winner by buying eggs from an Arab – when boiled and opened up, each egg contained a chicken.

A small stone cairn, similar to an Arab grave, stood nearby, so they went closer to investigate by looking in a crevice in the wall. The Bedouin and chico came up to them and tried to make them understand something about a South African corporal. They both thought an African corporal had been buried there. To make them understand better, the Arab drew in the sand a rabbit – the desert sands were a wonderful way to convey messages. It transpired that a South African corporal from Tobruk had brought back with him a rabbit, which quickly died in this land of starvation and the cairn had been its home. As the two airmen went on their way, they both glanced back at that little cairn, and the warm little story that it held for them – one crumb of comfort in a world at war.

They came upon the dried-up well in the *wadi*; the walls were of rock with a passage low down in the depths of the valley. The inevitable black beetles were crawling around at the bottom. They dropped a stone down the well, but there was no sound of water. The stone rolled under the passage out of sight; it was then they noticed a slight plop as it eventually found water. These subterranean passages fill up to the top in the rainy season but can barely last out till the next rain. They picked a few of the only visible flowers, a few anemones to put on their bedside locker of petrol tins. The gerbils hopped away on their long hind legs.

The men were getting weary of the monotonous diet, now only slightly relieved by tins of meat from a captured store of the Italians. These tins of meat were better than our tins as there were far more solid meat particles in them. Water as ever was in short supply, petrol seemed to be plentiful, so the airmen often washed their oily shorts in petrol. Once Alfred received a food parcel from home, but after the tin had been exposed to the boiling heat, when he opened it, everything was stuck together in a stinking mess – no more food parcels and no visiting entertainment parties.

7

Relief from Boredom

ALFRED decided to form his own entertainment committee to organise fancy dress shows, once again. These were to represent song titles, or book titles, with a present for the winner. The men had to make their costumes out of old tentage canvas, cardboard, paper and aircraft paint. As the entrants came forward into the marquee, the first person to recognise what the entrant represented was given a prize, which was also hard to come by in this land of shortages. These events were a great success and the medical officer remarked to Alfred that his shows did more good than all his medicine could achieve.

One night, sometime after 7 p.m., a sandstorm occurred which lasted throughout the night. It blew down most of the tents; Lofty Lowe's tent had completely disappeared, in its place was a mound of sand. At around six the following morning, there appeared a slight shimmering and shifting in the mound of sand. Eventually a voice was heard coming from that direction: 'What's up lads?' It was Lofty Lowe, who had refused to be disturbed by a mere sandstorm; his companions had earlier found shelter elsewhere. The cookhouse marquees were down in a heap of rubble. Much later in the day food was unearthed. The men tried to eat bully-beef sandwiches covered in sand; Alfred wondered if this was how sandwiches were first named. Many men had to have their ears syringed to rid them of small balls of sand.

General Rommel in the Western Desert

Suddenly the advance up the desert was to be reversed, after advance and retreat under Wavell, now under Auchinleck. Our commander seemed to be counteracting on orders of the day. Rommel now started his offensive to oust the Commonwealth forces from Egypt, or so he thought. Tobruk eventually fell.

Alfred was on the forward position of 203 Squadron beyond Gianaclis, another NCO and several African guards were on guard duty. At 2 a.m. they received orders over the phone, 'Retreat as quickly as possible, destroy all your ground equipment, unscrew the caps on the 40-gallon petrol drums.' But some spare wings of the Maryland aircraft were left intact. The African guards were new men straight from training in Africa, special care must be taken to get them away safely. Auchinleck in the meantime had advised the 8th Army to fall back to El-Alamein.

On 20 April 1942, records state that F/Sgt Moorhouse, Sgt Morgan, F/Sgt Martin and Sgt Murphy had set off at 16.57 hrs from Gianaclis to carry out a reconnaissance of the Sidi Barrani area, but failed to return (A/C Maryland 1640). The following day a plane was sent out to search for Maryland 1640, but with no result.

Alfred and his fellow NCO quickly complied with their order to retreat and they raced back to base camp. Alfred thought, is this the France-fiasco all over again? However, when they arrived back at base camp, all was pandemonium but, unlike the position in France, where there had been a shortage of vehicles, here was a surfeit to retreat with, but a shortage of drivers. Anyone with a modicum of driving skill was ordered to get in the cabs and join the retreating column down the desert road to a position on the desert midway between Alexandria and Cairo, known as Landing Ground X.

No sooner had Alfred parked his overheated vehicle, when he was ordered to retrace his journey with another NCO and the driver of a Queen Mary (articulated lorry) back to the place they had retreated from. The danger of capture was great indeed as they retraced their journey; signs were erected informing them to burn their vehicles should they lie in danger of capture. They were to try and salvage the wings of the Marylands that they had left behind, but when they got to the landing ground, there were clouds of dust disturbed by a tank battle that was now in progress. The tanks were manoeuvring into position for battle, when a Spitfire fell out of the sky and buried its port wing in the sand in front of their vehicle. The first thought that went through Alfred's mind was that it was the first Spitfire that he had seen since leaving England. They eventually found the wings of the Marylands and with the help of a tank crew (all full of admiration for the RAF) they loaded the wings in double-quick time on to the Queen Mary and departed. Never once did they think of turning back without accomplishing their allotted task. Alfred and his mate remarked on the bravery of the tank crews.

On 28 August 1942, at 13.07 hrs, it was officially recorded that P/O Harvey and W/O Underwood set off on a shipping reconnaissance to the south-west of Crete. The aircraft failed to return to base and no news was received of the crew (A/C Maryland 1666. A Sgt Macintosh also a member of the crew).

After a short space of time the forces began to build up and, in July 1942, they were ready for the great offensive. Up to this point Auchinleck had been afraid of losing Egypt and the Abadan oil supplies. The first offensive began on 13 July when General Alexander commanded Montgomery to go down to the desert and defeat Rommel, whose forces were now at the full extent of their supply lines; once again the position of the warring armies was reversed.

It was on 13 August that Montgomery assumed command of the 8th Army; he was so keen to get things sorted out that he counteracted orders and assumed command at an earlier date than that arranged for him. But he immediately made himself known to officers and men alike, a commander getting down to the feelings of men in the lower ranks. Immediately the spirits of the men were uplifted when they read on the notice-boards the new commanding officer's orders: 'We are to no more talk of retreating, and no talk of defeat. From now on we are going to advance and knock Rommel for six. We are getting new equipment and plenty of it!' He also immediately cut down on the rations of beer to one bottle per man per week: but

Alfred, running towards a crashed plane

now all the men thought of winning the campaign instead of losing one.

On 5 October 1942, a Blenheim T left on a training flight, but was not heard from again, according to records. Subsequent searches on 5, 6, and 7 October 1942 found nothing. The crew of Blenheim T were: Sgt Haley, P/O Henderson and Sgt Hunt.

The newer equipment that was now building up reassured Alfred and his mates; his mind went back to the days north of Berg-el-Arab when engines of Blenheims were only lasting a quarter of their allotted time, and the weather resulted in only one plane being serviceable.

A team of Volkes air-filter experts were sent to the squadron to try to improve on the air filters of the induction system against ever-increasing sandstorms. The chain operating the cooling fins ran through a circular metal ring around the engine. This got filled with dust and sand so that the hand-operated fins could no longer be worked. Alfred made a slight modification by boring a hole in the base of the ring; when syringed with paraffin it cleared the chain of sand.

On 11 October, at 12.48, records state that Lt Bergh, Sgt Hickson, Sgt Charlesworth and Sgt Mitchell set off from Giancalis on a shipping search to the west of Crete. The aircraft failed to return to base.

It was on 13 October that an SAS-type army of men entered the campaign to try to recapture Tobruk, but it was a failure.

There was now a build up of 300 new Sherman tanks just arrived from America and a build-up of the famous Spitfires and Hurricanes.

On 15 October, an entry in official records reveals that F/Sgt Flack and crew in Bisley E searched for a Baltimore which had failed to return to base following a patrol off the Palestine coast. A distress signal had been received from this aircraft and F/Sgt Flack located it on the beach in position 31° 04' N, 32° 45' E. The aircraft was burnt out... The following three members of the crew were eventually taken to Port Said by an RAF launch, in wounded conditions: F/Sgt Crombie, Sgt Lewers and Sgt Small. Sgt Todd was killed at the time of the accident.

On 23 October, all the men heard a mighty banging and crashing when 1,000 guns and 1,200 tanks opened up their mighty barrage. The noise was deafening, but music to the war-weary men who had been in the desert so long. In the battle the German Commander Stumme was killed. And now the first great battle of the war was being fought in earnest and El-Alamein was to be the first great success of the war. In the 9th Armoured Brigade engagement, they started with 132 tanks and lost 113.

In November, Rommel gave the order to withdraw from El-Alamein. Now it was time for 203 to advance once again. As they made their way up the desert road it was a sight to behold – the numerous shot-up and knocked-out tanks, the crashed aircraft on either side of the desert road as the fleeing enemy fanned out in a desperate effort to try to evade our planes and tanks.

A forced landing in the Western Desert

Every few hundred yards Italian CR 42 and CR 32s and German aircraft were to be seen lying about, shot up and burnt out. This was testimony to our Spitfires, Hurricanes and the many American planes engaged in this great battle. A far cry from battling on with the old Gladiators and other types of old planes. The Germans with their Conder aircraft of 1,000 miles' range were playing havoc with our ships at sea. In the 12 days battle there were 13,500 casualties and, to find another 13 – Brian Horrocks commanded 13 Corps at El-Alamein.

Alfred's tried and trusted friend for the last three years had been Sergeant Bond, who had flown to a forward position along with the air crew. Their plane was dual controlled; it got into difficulties, the other sergeant fitter was occupying the dual control position – did he try and take over control from the pilot? No one knows. However, they crashed, the Arabs ran to help the victims but Sergeant Bond died and so did the other fitter, but the pilot was saved (no record can be found in the operation books of this crash). Alfred was very upset for Sgt Bond had sailed out to the Middle East with him in the *Victory of India* (later sunk). He had once confided to Alfred:

'You know, Colonel, when I was at Hawkinge, a Lysander crashed and turned over and caught fire. I was near to it and saw the rear-gunner crawl out in great panic to get away from those enveloping flames. He had forgotten to unfasten his 'monkey strap' – length of wire with a release nozzle on the end which fastened between the legs. I rushed forward to try and release him but the flames beat me back. I sometimes have nightmares, hearing his screams and thinking that I could have done more to save him. I wonder if the same thing could happen to me?'

Now Sergeant Bond and his mate had met their fate in much the same circumstances.

Soon the squadron was to carry on with advancing. Christmas time was approaching and Alfred was determined to celebrate the event by organising a party. Many of his old contemporaries had left the Squadron, including Bill Groom, who, like himself was one of 13. Alfred thought that the *esprit de corps* of the squadron needed boosting up somewhat. So now a few volunteer helpers were organised to collect and save the odd bottles of beer of the non-drinkers' rations. On some occasions Alfred was allowed to fly to Alexandria with the air crew, so that he could obtain the odd crate of Stella beer.

As the advance was about to start again he got an NCO on each lorry to take charge of a crate of beer. Much was to be said for the conduct of the men and their abstinence of drink, that all the stock was safely unloaded at the advanced position in around 115° heat.

Each man was to contribute 50 piastres towards the forthcoming Christmas party. This was later increased to 70 piastres due to the increase in prices of stock. The storing of the Christmas stock became a problem, but fortunately this was overcome by obtaining an empty Spitfire crate. When they were dismantling it, Alfred was unscrewing the bottom side bolts and a man was aloft unscrewing the top bolts. The man aloft was told to stop unscrewing his bolts whilst Alfred got out of the way, but the message took too long to sink into his befuddled brain. The side of the huge crate started to bear down over the kneeling Alfred. Bending almost double he bolted away, the side of the crate bearing down on him. It finally caught his foot and pushed his toe into the soft sand, and the cushion of air steadied the huge side of the crate at the last moment.

Stella beer was obtained at 1.20 piastres, Crown at 96, and Australian at 48 per crate was 3.60 piastres. Spirits were obtained from the Officers' Mess. All this was guarded at night by Paddy Bonner and Alfred with rifle and bayonet.

The preparation for the Christmas party went ahead. Colonel often worked till 11 p.m., when he was off duty, building a bar out of cast-off material and petrol tins cut down into pieces. The only light was a hurricane lamp. Three hundred men eventually subscribed towards the party. As it drew nearer Christmas, the two marquees that were nearest to one another had the flaps joined together to make one big area – the enemy air attacks were now less frequent. The squadron artist was now employed in painting a picture across the front of the bar. There were no beer glasses so some bright spark thought up the idea of half filling beer bottles with liquid then inserting a red hot rod, which resulted in the neck of the bottle pulling off, with a slight tap. The lower half of the bottle, after rubbing down the sharp edges, was then ready to be used as a glass.

Darts match, mock football and tug-of-war games were organised. On opening night the bar was all laid out with stocks of beer and spirits – the spirits were mainly used to make cocktails. The cooks had done a wonderful job, with the aid of the men's subscriptions, in providing turkey rolls, ham sandwiches, buttered rolls, mince pies and twelve Christmas cakes, and cheese and pickles. This was a fantastic sight to see after such a long period of short rations.

A banner was erected across the entrance to the tents: 'Welcome to 203 Squadron's Christmas Party'. Wing Commander Grace, who was the CO, and the distinguished visitors, including Air Vice-Marshal Slaney, who cut the tape to declare the bar

An ammunition lorry on fire

open, arrived, and the men sang 'For He's a Jolly Good Fellow'. 'Colonel' and his team felt very proud to have organised the party against all odds. The squadron band and entertainers did a wonderful job. Everyone felt that they were not going to retreat again. But sad thoughts would creep into one's mind for those that were missing, never to return.

On the following Sunday a church service was held. 'Colonel' sent the following letter home:

Dear Mother,
In the marquee, boxes were made in the form of armchairs and a few forms were placed here and there. A table and piano formed the Padre's pulpit, in the background was the concert stage.

I had once met the Padre at the Toc H in Alexandria, he is a tall, finely built man of about forty-five years of age, with grey hair brushed back, which gave him a distinguished appearance, and he has kindly eyes which match his slight smile, for ever playing about the corners of his mouth.

He looked a typical country gentleman and his voice gave greater respect, for it was finely modulated and had a quiet fatherly air. He was of great contrast to the previous Padre who came like a business man, and conducted the service as an auctioneer would sell a cow.

I mused on the long dragging days, extended into months and then dragged on into years in the vast expanse of sand; it would be nice to get a little nearer to God through the aid of this Padre.

I noticed that Sgt Selby was there, a man who when on a week's leave in Alexandria, would be drunk from noon till morn, he had come to this service to find again his innermost self.

The Padre said he had given up his parish in England to come out here to give hope and comfort to those forgotten men of the desert. He felt that the Christian religion was greatly needed in these trying times. He stressed the point of conduct of the people of the first Great War, of immorality, and the indifferent attitude to religion, when the regular churchgoers were laughed at as being old fashioned But if a thing was proved good it was well worth sticking to it.

I thought of the complex nature of things, why was I in the RAF? We are also responsible for killing people.

But I believe that force is the only alternative on certain occasions, to overcome evil such as that madman Hitler. Wars are such complex things to deal with, I feel sorry for the Commanders who have to make such far reaching decisions in regard to men's lives.

My reverie was interrupted by the Padre asking if anyone preferred a hymn. On opening my hymn book I saw 'Oh God our help in ages past'.

I remember that you, Mother, also hummed that tune back on the farm, all those thousands of miles away. The Padre was pleased for it seemed to fit in with his service.

I also felt that in the adversities of life in warfare, the more temperate of men were better able to pass on some of

The opening of the Christmas party, 1943.
(*From left*) Wing Commander Grace, Air Vice-Marshal Slaney
and Adjutant

Italian prisoners surrendering

the inner goodness that was still left in one. Also to temper
down the more aggressive nature of some men.

Japan at war, Germany and Italy have declared war on
America. The world has now been at war several months –
we need God's help.
Your loving son
Alfred

Streams of Italian and German prisoners of war were now
wearily wending their way down the Desert Road. Some of them
were picked up in 203 Squadron vehicles to take them to the
camps. The Italians looked relieved and subdued, they were
mainly pleased that the war for them had ended. The German
prisoners of war were glum-faced and more aggressive looking,
for only a few weeks ago they were being told that Egypt was
theirs for the picking.

As the lorries filled up with the Italian prisoners, their guards

The new supply of Bostons to 203 Squadron. (*Back row, from left*) McCloud, Robson, Ford, Booth, Blatherwick, Reen, Scholes; (*second row*) Hinchcliffe, Wright, Farral, Smith, Harvey, ?, Steel, Lawson, Fudge, Cockton, ?, Smith, ?; (*third row*) Dye, Hall, Dawson, Cpl Campbell, Flt Sgt Campbell, Sqn Ldr Woolley, ?, Barker, Basnett, Remnent, Martingstall, ?; (*front row*) ?, ?, Bowes, Beech, Ramsey, Wilkinson, East, Jones, Miller, Campbell with rifles and bayonets still standing below them, nonchalantly handed them up to them whilst they clambered aboard. Alfred thought it the most amusing thing for the guard to hand his rifle and bayonet to a prisoner of war. It turned out that their guard was an East End lad of Italian blood himself. He was speaking to them in Italian – he was probably telling them to come to London and sell ice-cream.

The order now came through for 203 Squadron to make a long endurance trip of about 850 miles to Benghazi in the Libyan Desert. As the convoy advanced in open and covered lorries they wended their way through the famous battle names of El-Daba, Fuka Matruh, Sidi Barrani and Solum. Tobruk they skirted by travelling on the bypass road, constructed by the Italians and Germans when the Commonwealth forces held the fort for so long. They travelled over Solum Pass and Hell Fire Pass which had previously been bombed every quarter-hour to dislodge the enemy. The winding road around the hills of Tocra Pass was hazardous as the enemy had blown up parts of the roads and bridges around the pass. Several tanks were lying far down below after being blown off the narrow roads.

Suddenly a new world opened up to the men, when they pulled up the vehicles for bivouac on the Jebel Akhdar – which means green mountains. Trees and grass and scores of wild flowers. After years in the desert of sandstorms and no relief to blinding heat, the men just rolled about in the luscious greenery, lovingly picking a different-coloured flower from here and there. The abandonment of the men reminded Alfred of the days back on the farm, when young gambolling stock were turned out of doors for the very first time. There were blood red patches of poppies, then the lighter blue of thousands of bird's eye, then patches of white dog daisies, and millions of anemones amid other smaller flowers whose great number transformed the mountainous countryside into a multi-coloured panorama, most pleasing to the eye. It was truly great to see hills and rocks and areas of grass again.

Alfred now noticed the convoy was taking up position again, so he hurried back to clamber aboard. He felt that he was leaving a little of his heart back there in that clearing on the hills of Jebel Akhdar.

In the green Jebel Hills, with the Advance Party

The men had been warned to try and be friendly with any natives they should come in contact with as they neared Apollonia. For this had been Mussolini's Headquarters in North Africa. As they were eating their meal, made up from Italian tins of meat, two Arab men approached them in a friendly manner. LAC Fulger, who had just been made a member of the newly formed RAF Regiment and was issued with a tommy-gun, jumped up from where he had been sitting on the ground and taking aim with his newly acquired gun, he threatened to shoot the two men. In his brand new ego as a trooper, it was quite possible that he may have fired the gun.

Alfred was quick to react by jumping in front of the two natives and, facing LAC Fulger, shouted: 'If you shoot at them, then you've got to shoot me first.' Common sense prevailed, Alfred gave Fulger a good ticking off and threatened him with a

The two Arabs who were threatened by Fulger and his tommy-gun
before Alfred intervened

charge should he do anything so stupid again. He reflected on
the last letter he had sent home and his remarks on tempering
down the more aggressive nature of man.

Eventually, in March 1943, they arrived at Berka 3 near
Benghazi, which had been their old base in their first advance.
The 8th Army and advanced Desert Air Force had already got to
Tripoli on 15 January that year. Things seemed to be going well
now towards the end of the Desert Campaign and Thank God,
thought Alfred, with his mixed feelings of self pity, but compassion for others after years of privation in this sand-happy world.
One's own creative ability had been so restricted in this tightly
controlled military existence. Thank the Lord that his friend
Ernie Campbell, although promoted to sergeant, was still with
them.

In his letter to his mother he wrote:

My reflections are on the events of the last two and a half years of desert life. Letter writing seems more difficult to concentrate upon particularly as regards to what one can or cannot say to get by the censor's restrictions.

Whilst the first great battle of the war was being fought the men felt that all the world's eyes were upon them. Especially the people at home; one could not let them down, the battle had to be won at all cost. Our admiration goes out to that great Herculean effort on the most heavily bombed place on Earth – Malta's people and our efforts to keep them going.

Many of our squadron men and planes have been lost in seas around the area. But now that it almost over the stalemate has set in.

As the lines of communication grew longer and shipping space more scarce, even little luxuries were cut out.

One bottle of beer per week, occasionally two. Soft drinks such as lemonade has been off the ration for long periods. One brand of cigarettes, one brand of pipe tobacco, one tin of fruit between 10 men. One razor blade between two men per week and one tablet of soap between four men per week. Food rations were at a minimum. But now the food is much better, we have dinner at 6.30 p.m. but it is so hot, one sits in the dining tent, the perspiration runs down one's arms on to the table, from there it drips onto the knees.

Then as one drinks more of the mug of brackish tea one can feel trickles running down the back. Finally one slings down the knife and fork to let the perspiration take its shortest course to the ground.

The beneficial side of sweating is that all the built-up dirt comes out of the open pores. Close to this area it was registered as 130°F, which is very hot indeed.

After years of being in different phases of the war, and in the fatiguing sandstorms of the deserts, I feel that quite a few of us are getting just a little war weary, it would be nice to see and hear the opposite sex for change.

As I write this letter the invasion of Sicily has just started, but it was not news for us for we could see the ships going along from our seaward view.

Anything startling which takes place now, does not seem to quicken the pulses and to get the adrenaline flowing as it used to do.

We now take things more as a matter of course.

Your loving son

Alfred

Some of the men were sent to Apollonia on a week's recuperation where they were billeted in an ex-army camp of Mussolini's. They particularly admired the fountain structure that Mussolini had erected in the square. The great amphitheatre of the old Roman Empire was of great interest to the men. Alfred's mind wandered over the centuries and reminisced on the historical period when the Romans had occupied Britain. Our money, our measurement had been based on their teachings. One could not really imagine them to be our enemy over a long period of time, for so many of them had settled in our country over the years.

The men were allowed to visit Benghazi in off duty hours. Mussolini had settled some of the Africans from his southern part of his new empire, building into this region. This has caused animosity particularly amongst the Senussi tribe; now the Commonwealth troops were picking up the tasks of policing the country.

Alfred's police chief of earlier days was now here to be in charge of civil duties: he was Captain Rawlings of the Derby Force.

As the men had been instructed to be as friendly as possible with the natives of the area, Alfred and his mates were complying with their instructions. On returning to camp after an evening in town, they were quietly passing the local mosque. It always gave Alfred a feeling of respect when the dignified figure of the Muslim priest circuited the minaret of the mosque, his strident voice calling down below to come to prayer at 10 p.m. in the evening: *Yo Mohamid Talyerhena, Alla-Alla.*

Sure enough, spot on the hour, the priest circuited the minaret but instead of the jellaba-clad figure of the priest, with his strident voice, another loud and clear voice rang out: 'She'll Be Coming Round The Mountain When She Comes!' An inebriated soldier had found his way up on to the minaret, but he was quickly ejected by the Arabs. Alfred thought this little episode was typical of the British character, of wanting to be part of an act. But was it not much better than being armed and wanting to shoot at everything that moved?

The neighbouring squadron at Berka 3 was the American 600 Squadron which was part of 398 Bombardment Group. They were on intensive training to take part in the bombing of the Romanian oil wells. One of their Flying Fortresses was just taking off when the starboard engine burst into flames and the pilot sheered left to try to land. The plane was heading towards the tents where Alfred and AC Blatherwick were, after being on the previous night's guard duty.

Suddenly they heard the engine starting to backfire and they rushed out of their tent and saw that the pilot was making a forced landing close by. It was soft sand and sand dunes in the area and the huge monster touched ground, careered for a few hundred yards or more beyond the tents. Alfred and Blatherwick rushed towards the plane. As they ran, they saw the nose of the huge monster dig into the sand, then the tail gradually rose into the air to a perpendicular position. It looked like some great monster from outer space biting at the earth beneath it. For a few moments it stood poised, its tail pointing skywards; then the even pull of gravity gradually was overcome by the inertia of petrol forcing the plane to complete its half circle to fall on its back.

Alfred and AC Blatherwick were the first persons to try to help the crew escape. One man had already crawled out and then dashed back into the burning wreck to try to rescue his comrades. Alfred and Blatherwick dashed forward to enter the fuselage, but all that they could see were piles of upturned equipment, they were unable to find anyone else.

The medical officer and others now rushed up to the scene, shouting for the men to come away as they thought the plane was bombed up and would explode at any moment. It was later believed that an airman was trapped under the nose of the plane but he would have been killed on impact with the ground. There is no greater horror than to see a crash of flaming wreckage and being unable to do much about it.

Alfred wrote home to explain the changing conditions in Benghazi now that the constant bombing of the town had eventually ceased:

> The town of Benghazi after many bombings is now in the process of being cleared by the Arabs. Many homes have been reduced to heaps of rubble, others left in fantastic shapes, with walls missing here and there disclosing the floors of the bedrooms on which articles of furniture still remain, so reminiscent of other areas of war. The floor of the upper storey of a printing house had collapsed on to the printing machines, which awaits salvage and reconstruction. Practically every building in the town has suffered from the terrific bombardment of three years of war. The shrapnel-spotted walls are being patched up.
>
> The former Greek, French and Italians are re-opening up cafés and restaurants. Lorries are coming down from Libya piled up with repatriated Arabs and Italians. The USA and Commonwealth troops visit the restaurants where chicken (old boiler), tomato and egg – often half bad – bread and coffee costs twenty piastres.
>
> The cinema is roofless, the rubble has been cleared away. Film shows are now operating again with the sky as a canopy.
>
> Mussolini's huge portrait is still clinging to the wall, he is staring down on his conquerors with unseeing eyes.
>
> Your loving son.

The squadron sustained no casualties during September 1943. But news was received that Lt H. W. Nottingham, SAAF, who was reported missing on 10 July last from an offensive operation off Crete, was taken prisoner the same day and died in hospital

These five brave men had just dropped supplies to five men at sea

on 13 July. Nothing more is known of his crew, Sgt Donner, Sgt Oldham, AE and F/Sgt Roberts ASRNZAF, who are reported missing.

On the Monday Alfred received a very nice letter from Sergeant Bond's parents, in reply to his earlier commiseration with them, on the death of their beloved son. They asked him to visit them, when the war was over, but at this stage no firm commitment could be undertaken.

Every time the squadron moved there seemed to be a plague of some kind or other. First there was a plague of bugs, then fleas, then mosquitoes and now a great plague of beetles – thousands of them to every square foot of the desert. They reminded Alfred of the plague of June beetles when in France with the Expeditionary Force. Did these things occur by the uneven cycle of evolution caused by war, he wondered?

There were two Bedouin women squatting on their heels opposite each other, one had a big stick, the other a mallet. With these implements, they were beating a heap of straw. They were

Farnell, a Canadian, as 'God Bless America',
wearing a horse's tail for a beard

Remnent and Martin as 'The Organ, the Monkey and Me'

Bert Clay as 'Burlington Bertie'

threshing much as their ancestors had done for over thousands of years. With the corn they made chapatties, beaten up into flour and mixed into paste with eggs and water, and then laid in big pancakes on the ashes of the open hearth to bake. This is the staple diet of Bedouin Arabs.

An occasional Arab farmer drove his mule and now rubber-wheeled cart to his homestead. The Arabs have been quick to seize the opportunity of a little looting from vehicles cast off by the foreign armies as they moved back and forth over their beloved land. Perhaps the Arabs are the real profiteers of these warring armies who seem hell bent on destroying one another. They have sat tight on their patch regularly bending forth on knees, facing east, to pray to Allah. They have befriended each victorious army in turn, knowing that in the end they would be the actual winners.

On 5 October 1943, it was recorded that at 07.10 W/O H. W. Robinson, F/Lt P. A. Gwyne, F/Sgt G. W. Bridgewater and R. R. Doddington were airborne on a photo recce of the Central Aegean. The RDF plot lost trace of the aircraft on the outward journey at the customary range but no further signal or news was received and the crew were presumed missing . . .

Another noticeboard announcement, asking for volunteer NCOs for dangerous duties: a fed-up, stalemated Corporal Alfred again applied but his application form was once again torn up. He now seemed a permanent fixture of 203 Squadron. Once again he started to organise fancy dress shows along with a volunteer team. The men were getting very bored, now that the 8th Army had left them for their battles elsewhere.

Some months earlier, on 13 May 1943, General Alexander had sent Churchill a message that the Tunisian Campaign was now over. The King had also sent a message on 13th to congratulate Churchill on the victory. Two hundred and forty-eight thousand prisoners had been taken by our troops, but still 203 Squadron were losing men and planes. Many of Alfred's mates were now posted from the squadron or had lost their lives.

Alfred was always fascinated with the men's own inspiration on designing the fancy dresses, practically out of thin air, old tentage and paint for costumes, and rope combed out for hair.

On one occasion a beard was needed for 'God Bless America'. An Arab horse was chased and caught to have a piece of its tail cut off for the beard of 'God Bless America', and to top up the strangeness of the situation, the man who acted the part was a

Benniwith as 'Snake Charmer from Old Baghdad'

Canadian. LAC Benniwith was particularly good as the 'Snake Charmer of Old Baghdad' – he had used old heater pipes discarded from aircraft, which were bent into shapes to represent rising snakes. Cocoa gave him a darker complexion to make him look more like an Arab. 'You are my heart's desire', with Sergeant Campbell as the bottle of beer, and Flight Sergeant Campbell as a drunk, leaning on the bottle for support, was excellent.

Remnent was dressed up as 'The Organ, the Monkey and Me' with Martin wearing a flying jacket as the monkey, and Charlie Pether, a Maltese chap, was very good in his make-up as 'Carmen Miranda'.

Prizes were hard to come by. Alfred approached the Americans of 600 Bomber Squadron. They were superb in providing bottles of whisky, gin and other bottles of spirits at cost price and these were given out as prizes for the best costume representing song or book titles. The first person in the audience to guess who the participants represented also got a prize. They were a great success and helped to relieve the boredom of the men.

On 18 October, records indicate that F/O D. K. Mennell and crew were briefed to carry out a photo recce of COS from Gambut 3. As they took off at dawn the port motor cut out and F/O Mennell skilfully ground looped to avoid running into some domestic lines. The aircraft broke in two aft of the main spar and came to rest with forward half upside down. The navigator, F/O A. T. Leydin, RAAF, was killed outright, F/O Mennell and F/Lt A. D. Nourse, RAAF, the Squadron Gunnery and Signals Officer, were injured and taken to hospital, and F/Sgt Salvidge, who was in the wireless operator's place escaped with slight cuts.

At 09.30 on 1 November, it was recorded that F/Sgt T. Withers, F/O D. Watson, F/Sgt B. H. Gibbon and F/Sgt W. J. Hall were airborne for a photo recce of the Central Aegean in fair weather. No signal or news was received of this crew and they were presumed missing.

Alfred now noticed that he had developed an infected swollen lump under his right forearm which had entered the blood vessel with poison. He reported to the sick tent where a Palestinian medical orderly took one look at it and then commenced to squeeze all the pus out of it. There was no pussy footing attitude with the medic, who squeezed with all his might and Alfred

Pigge as 'Minnie the Moocher'

Martingstall and Booth as 'Dr Livingstone'

thought that part of his forearm was going to be squeezed out through the wound. After dressing it he was told to occupy a bed in the sick tent for a week. One day was enough for Alfred and he discharged himself and went back to work.

Wing Commander Masterman was now the commanding officer. He was an ex-Guardsman, and a man of stature; his predecessor, Wing Commander Grace, had been a bit laid back in comparison.

Perhaps the squadron was due for change in the near future; the planes were now standing idle on the dispersal points. A new plague of locusts covered them; when one periodically ran the engines up for testing – and for something to do – the swirling blades of the propellers kill millions. The engines got covered in a thick layer of the mangled-up bodies of the beastly things.

For something better to do, Alfred wrote a long letter to his mother:

Dear Mother,
Recently I have received much mail from you. I am very pleased to hear you are all well and happy. We are at present in limbo, the planes are standing idle, some of us are experiencing conflicting emotions. Depression has set in, followed by short spells of high spirits.

We describe it as 'sandhappy', so this is the reason why I organise fancy-dress shows with our committee. We have been on the 'blue' for too long now, we desire a change, little jealousies with some men and introverts with others, who seem to have no interests beyond themselves.

We have carried on too long with only the bare necessities of life. Camp environment is the only thing we know, our thoughts often turn to home and family life, but in moments of stress the better part of the mind comes to one's rescue, so protecting the mortal soul it controls. Others will find some form of trivial hobby to relieve the boredom.

Most of us are from families whose parents were brought up in the Christian faith, many of the men are virgins waiting for the day when they can meet up with a girl of their dreams.

The hardest hit are those who are married. The war with its terrible, bloody trimmings grinds on relentlessly. But out of all this springs good friendships between men, surprising in its solidarity and understanding of each other.

Perhaps I am writing in this vein because four of us always knocked about together. One was Sergeant Bond who was killed, Bill Groom, who has been sent back to England and John Murdock, who has just been posted from us. But I still remain on this old overseas squadron trying to maintain the *esprit de corps*.

Sgt Bond was the one who always made fun, yet could be serious as occasion demanded it. Bill Groom was one of the youngest, yet the oldest in organising ability for the betterment of the squadron. John Murdock was the irresponsible one of the party; but always in good spirits, never offended.

On the whole the men are a wonderful crowd of chaps. I feel honoured to have served with them. We think we have done our lot for the Freedom of Mankind. We have suffered together, or enjoyed together, the life that we have been forced to live.

As I write this letter the sound of a male voice choir, struck my ears; I remembered there was a service in the Marquee. The singing of hymns and seeing the most unlikely faces there greatly relieves the pent-up feelings of our imprisoned existence. As the men come away from the service they seem to talk in a freer, lighter voice.

I wonder what the Padres think of us? Some of them are military padres, others have been vicars in quiet little parishes, who have left them behind to come amongst us. They are probably surprised at the low attendance, but those men who do attend the service greatly appreciate the Padre and his lesson.

Now as one walks across the great plain, stretching away into the distance to meet the sky, and the great silky clouds

Norman Wright, with Wilkinson, Remnent, Smith, Dawson and Martin as 'The Five Quins'

rolling gently over the sun, and the shadows gently chasing each successive desert bush, until even they seem too lazy and are overcome by the suns burning rays – all is well with the world. But for how long?

The squadron is gradually turning over to Wellington aircraft, I think we shall soon be on the move.

At 16.00 hours on 5 November 1943, according to official records, F/Lt R. G. Fox, RAAF, was carrying out local solo flying practice at LG 91, in a Wellington aircraft. Shortly after taking off the aircraft was seen to dive to the ground and crash. F/Lt Fox was killed and the cause of the accident was unknown.

In another letter home, Alfred wrote:

Dear Mother,
The mud huts of the Arab shepherds take on fantastic shapes in the shimmering heat of the mirage, like some prehistoric monster, dancing a queer step.

The enormity of the universe is suddenly in strict contrast to minute life on earth, as one looks down on the buzzing insects and sparse plant life of the desert.

On such occasions, no where else, only on the desert, standing all alone, can one feel the pure peacefulness and warming quietude after one of these Padre's services. One then realises that most of the present day's world-wide strife is man-made. You then feel that the earth's elements are far more easy to deal with than the man-made trauma of horror. As one then turns back towards camp, the feelings completely change, a slightly rebellious mood overcomes one. Why go back to an insane world?

These are the moods we get into over here, but no doubt on quieter reflection, I should probably have torn this letter up. But my thoughts must come out.

One of our great battles out here seems to be with the mastering of oneself against the monotony and deprivation from a normal civilised world.

The poor Arab struggling to grow his sparse crop of maize has already faced droughts and destroying sandstorms. Now he has the worst enemy of them all; the Arab women can be seen with wands thrashing amongst the slender crop in a vain effort to drive the locusts away. They rise in swarms, like black hovering clouds only to land again in their endeavour to consume every green shoot in sight.

As I have once said in my earlier letters – the Arab must be the world's number one optimist. On commiserating with the Arabs, they said that the locusts would disappear on the 15th to 16th of June. Almost to the day they started to fly off inland.

Your loving son.

Now it is longer stretches of inaction, followed by longer stretches of monotony, interspersed with short visits to troop-crowded towns. The civilian native shopkeeper obligingly relieves one of hard-saved money in the shortest possible time. Quite a number of young men were engaged to get married before leaving England. Often a letter arrives from the 'queen' they left behind. When you walk into a tent there you will see a photograph on a box or tin can, or hung up on the tent canvas wall – it is a picture of his girl. He comes into the tent in the evening, sorts about in his ditty-box and pulls out some souvenir

Charlie Pether as 'Carmen Miranda'

Sergeant Campbell in costume and Flight Sergeant Campbell
as 'You Are My Heart's Desire

Cigarette case presented to Corporal Barker by 203 Squadron

which has taken his fancy. He looks at it with pride and tells you how he will present it to his girl when he gets back, for she has promised – come what may – that she will always love him and wait for him.

He then gets a 'Dear John' letter in the morning post. Waiting anxiously for his name to be called, he takes a quick look at the familiar handwriting, tears the letter open with trembling hands, but in a few seconds his face alters from a picture of bliss to one of disbelieving anger. The corners of his mouth droop, the letter is quickly folded up and pocketed. When you speak to him, he answers you abstractedly. The boys chide him – 'Another letter eh!'

He had read: 'Many thanks for your beautiful letter and photograph. The times out there must be very trying for you. I have met a very nice boy who went to school with you, I am sure you will like him. We were engaged to be married last week, but I still love etc...' He enters his tent, the photograph of his girl is quietly taken down and a beer bottle is put on his locker in its place. He is a very subdued man for some weeks.

Finally, relief came in the guise of a DC3 plane; Alfred with an advance party took off for landing ground 91, some three and a half hours' flying time away. As they circled the Marylands and

Baltimores below them, Alfred wondered what their future, with their locust-splattered engine, would be. At landing 75.0 T U there was a great reunion of chaps of old, then a split up again: the final end of 203 Squadron in the Middle East.

8

Flight to India

NOW there were new Wellington bombers awaiting to fly the squadron to India. In the completely new makeup of 203 Squadron, 'Colonel' Cpl Barker was chosen to fly as Flight Engineer on Wing Commander Masterman's crew in Wellington M765.

Corporal Barker (*centre*), Blondy Pearce (*right*) and crew as they flew from the Western Desert to India

Their first call was Habanya. In the morning, when Alfred was inspecting and testing the engines, he discovered a magneto drop in revolution on the starboard engine. The contact breaker block was seized on its axis. When inquiring at base camp for a spare unit, the local sergeant fitter turned out to be Bill Brennan – this was the third time of meeting up with his old friend of the Spitfire days at Duxford. He soon issued Alfred with a new contact breaker block.

It was now time for take off and there was a lot of extra equipment on the plane making it extra heavy. Wellington M765 was now racing down the runway and had almost reached take-off speed when a red Verey light was fired across their bows. This is it! thought the crew as they were ordered to gather together in the centre of the plane. Wing Commander Masterman throttled back, the plane rushed forward. There seemed little hope of avoiding going through the perimeter fence and the dangers beyond – of the plane smashing up and bursting into flames. But the plane swung round, narrowly missing having its wing torn off. Apparently a plane was attempting to land that was out of fuel and the two planes had crossed, one in the air and the other taking off. A little later, after a successful take off, they flew on to Bahrain and then to Karachi in India. It was nearing the monsoon season, the atmosphere was very sticky; where everywhere was now brown, it would soon be transformed into green vegetation and the baked earth would be a quagmire of mud. The heat was now terrific, and the sky was becoming overcast, ominous of the impending rains.

On 12 November 1943, at the height of Gandhi's career, they landed at Santa Cruz near Bombay. Gandhi's headquarters were at the beach hut at Juhu beach.

Every morning at 7 a.m. as it was breaking daylight, millions of crows and kites collect from the forests and fly overhead making a tremendous croaking row, warning each other of their presence in the grey heavens. The vultures perch wherever it is convenient, poking their heads this way and that way in an endeavour to obtain a better view, and the opportunity of stealing unguarded food. In the clear sky the following day was a huge circle of vultures, spiralling down to earth like a squadron of bombers – a sight not to be forgotten. The vultures, or *assvogels* as our South Africans call them, stand around in a circle, their big wing muscles prominent like the shoulder muscles of some prize fighter. Long, lean, scraggy necks, with a wicked featherless head, and beady eyes and hook beak. Feathered legs with huge razor sharp talons, with which they scratch and tear pieces of meat from the corpse. A great battle suddenly starts as a new member alights. Cruel spurs are sunk into flesh or sinew, the curved beaks are used, anything to get at that carcass, so that the fittest may survive. In a short time, white bones and skulking pye-dogs are all that remain in the blazing sun.

Meanwhile the spoilers are sunning themselves high up in the palm trees; their wings spread vertically outwards resembling the Italian badge-eagle. They are visible from several miles away, like great crosses on a totem pole. Others are up in the heavens again, gliding, rising and falling on the ever-prevalent air currents. The most beautiful gliders to be possessed of wings, they never seem to move a muscle. Every air current is known to them and used to the full advantage, their eyes for ever glued to the ground below them. The sign of a faltering step, or weary body, is a suspicion of death on earth, in their hungry eyes.

In the adjoining woods at Santa Cruz is a little church with a Portuguese priest, who has a few Portuguese in his congregation, probably the remaining beings from the former Portuguese colony. On entering the wood Alfred came across two very large and well built wells which had been made by the colony. One was dated 184 something and the other 1919. All over the place were crosses with INRI printed on them. It was known as the place of the Holy Cross.

Beer is even more scarce here than in the desert, it is only served in the canteen once a month and no beer is sold outside in the towns. Some restaurants sell spirits. The Wayside Inn was 203 Squadron's visiting place in Bombay.

Back at camp their sleeping quarters were made of bamboo poles and covered with rush. The yellow transparent ants were busy making mucus to stick on the poles so that they could work

underneath to eat away the woodwork. The natives were constantly on their rounds, banging with their sticks on to the poles
to dislodge the ants. Millions of mosquitoes found their way
under the mosquito nets, irrespective of how one tucked the nets
under the bed. Fortunately there are not so many malaria species
as those in Egypt.

Our furry friend, the mongoose, suddenly finds his way under
the tucked-in edge of the mosquito net. He settles down on
the bed – one of the flying crews had befriended the little
animal. This was surprising as all the natives seem to run
away from them. It was fantastic to watch the mongoose kill
a snake – the natives seem to think that's what we keep him
for. But he is a great friend of all the men. When the squadron
moves he flies in one of the planes, which has to be a little
lower than normal, for the little fellow can't stand the higher
altitudes.

Alfred was now one of the senior members of 203 Squadron
wartime service, most of the men having left the squadron and
new ones taking their place. He had served under Wing
Commander Johnson, Wing Commander Grace and now Wing
Commander Masterman. He admired the methods of his
present C/O in trying to maintain the *esprit de corps* of the
squadron.

One day the men were busy working on the Wellington when
W/C Masterman suddenly appeared and ordered Corporal
Barker and other NCOs to gather the men together to form into
line for inspection.

Two very important and extremely handsome men arrived:
Earl Mountbatten and Douglas Fairbanks Junior. Earl Mountbatten ordered the men to gather round in a circle so that he
could talk to them. Douglas Fairbanks was in the uniform of a
colonel, for he had been made an honorary colonel of the
American Forces. They looked a very handsome pair of men, on
the world stage of history making. Alfred and his mates were part
of this; they were here to help prepare India for self-rule, but
probably many of them did not realise this at the time. The great
Empire, almost quartering the world, was in the process of
coming to an end. Alfred felt that it would be a wonderful thing

if this great continent of India could be as one, but forthcoming events had not yet taken their toll.

Back in England, on 13 June the Germans had released their Doodlebugs on to Britain.

Wing Commander Masterman had already sent for 'the Colonel' as he called Alfred and said, 'You've always done the welfare on the squadron, Corporal Barker, so you can carry on and form a proper canteen and entertainment for the men. I have ordered an officer to help you in this respect.' The welfare officer turned out to be the young Lord Walpole.

Volunteer workers for welfare proved hard to win over, but eventually a small hard-working team provided a tented library and canteen. They knew they would not be advancing and retreating as they had done in the desert.

An important little person in the form of the prognostic Gandhi now came to visit Bombay, staying in his hut nearby. The natives working for the RAF squadron went on 'go-slow' tactics in sympathy to the obedience of Gandhi's wishes. There was to be no violence, but to just show that the occupation of their country could no longer to be tolerated. But there was a strong bond between some of their servicemen and ours. Had they not just proved themselves as some of the finest units in the Western Desert Campaign and in other areas of war?

Gandhi was remarkable in the power that he held, by means of 'no violence' in his teachings. He held respect from his own people, as well as admiration from the occupiers of his country. But this vast continent, with its multitude of humanity of so many differing creeds and cultures, would need more than one ruler.

The British had left their mark on India, as the Roman occupiers of Britain had done some two thousand years before. The second greatest railway in the world ran across the Indian continent, built under the supervision of the British. The common language of English could cut through the differing dialects.

But now the Indian nation was intent on home rule. One evening when Alfred had paid a visit to Bombay he was walking back towards camp, when he met an RAF squadron leader who turned out to be his sergeant of Spitfire days at Duxford. He had always admired Sergeant Chapman as a fair and dedicated NCO. His new rank did not surprise Alfred and he wished the now squadron leader well for the future.

'What do you think of India, Cpl Barker?'

'Oh! so much different from my experience of Egypt and Libya. The Indians are such hard-working people, including all the family, and the culture is so fascinating, I hope when we leave the country that peace can prevail.'

Squadron Leader Chapman seemed unwilling for further conversation on this score, so they exchanged pleasantries with one another and proceeded on their different ways.

Alfred was later stopped as he walked down the street, by several Indians in a motorcar.

'Would you like a lift back to your drome, Corporal?' said the driver.

'Thank you very much, gentlemen, I will gladly accept the offer.'

As they drove off, the Indians were keen to start up a conversation. 'Do you like India, Corporal? Don't take too much notice of the graffiti on the walls, telling the British to get out of India. We are all worried, for while you are here, you try to keep the peace. But when, or if, you go, goodness knows what will happen.' The love-hate relationship with Britain still existed, it seemed.

A short time after this incident Alfred flew on a detachment to Rawalpindi on the North-West Frontier. It seemed we were trying to make ourselves appear well equipped should there be threat of invasion by Russia on the one hand and Japan on the other. The landing ground lay in a basin which was almost surrounded by mountains of the North-West Frontier. Around seven o'clock in the evening great black clouds gathered above and around the basin, ever closing inwards as the day's heat evaporated in the cooling air above. This left a vacuum for the incoming colder air.

Suddenly the huge, thick black clouds met head on. Great sheets of lightning, way up in the universe, flashed their zigzag course down to earth, followed by ear-splitting crashes of thunder as if one was trying to prove it was mightier than the other.

Flying aircraft on these occasions was ruled out, one would stand and wonder which aircraft on the ground would be the victim of those tremendous zigzag flashes.

A party of men was sent to collect some string-based beds from the Indian peasants. As an airman was directing the stacking of the beds on the lorry, he found he had an irritating seed under his dentures. He took the dentures out and one of the natives standing below him looked up in amazement and shouted to his mates, while pointing to this foreigner who could take his teeth out and put them back again. They then indicated to Alfred to take his teeth out, but he had to show them that his teeth were fixed and no matter how hard he pulled at them, they would not come out. Alfred mused on the white man's fascination with the natives' exploding universe, whilst they were fascinated by the white men being able to remove their teeth.

In January, on their return to Santa Cruz, the senior corporals were dispatched to Secunderabad to go on a senior NCOs course. This was held in the Maharajah's palace, which he had turned over for the use of Indian and colonial troops. Much of the rear structure of the palace was undermined by huge rodents which could be seen disappearing down the large holes followed by their never ending tails. The large pillared, bathing pool lined with marble, was now empty of water.

The parade ground and military huts were forever busy, the troops spick and span, in this great effort to prepare for the home rule of India.

The NCOs of 203 Squadron, having been used to rather free and easy desert life, where parades and drilling would have been impossible in sandstorms, were now expected to conform to the stricter, smarter parade-ground disciplines. Corporal Barker, ever proud of his squadron's accomplishments and *esprit de corps* of his unit, felt the time was ripe to gather the NCOs together to suggest that everyone should do their utmost to make the entry one of the best.

Surprisingly, everyone agreed. They were very fortunate in having some of the best No 1 Grade Warrant Officers and Senior NCOs as instructors in the whole of the RAF. They passed out with higher marks than all former entries, much to the delight of Wing Commander Masterman, who complimented Corporal Barker on their return to the squadron.

On the course the Indian and British men were encouraged to have discussions for the future home rule of India. One or two of the Indians had been subjected to Japanese propaganda. Alfred and his mates quickly argued that it would be silly to let the Japanese into the country, when it was so evident that Britain was pulling out of India.

Britain had always been aware of the covetous eyes of Russia and now the more immediate threat of Japan. In his reflective state of mind Alfred decided to take a walk on his own – he liked to ponder on the world's situation in his leisurely walks, during odd hours of release from duty. He wandered over the hills and rocks in the wilder part of the district. He disturbed some partridges which took to flight in front of him. He thought they looked smaller than the English variety. As he climbed some high rocks, he stopped and stood and viewed the scenery below him, he felt the solitariness of one small human being amongst a wilderness of giant rocks. A lovely breeze began to blow, gently wafting across his brow. He could see the camp in the distance; what a relief to get away from that monotonous environment for a while.

A squirrel suddenly scampered across his path; with bushy tail outstretched, he made convulsive jumps to climb a big rock and was soon lost to view. A small bird flew by and settled on to the top of a protruding ridge of stone. Slowly but surely she hopped her way forward until she reached her objective. It was a small fissure in the rock face, she quickly popped food into the hungry open beaks of her young, whilst the cock bird was ever vigilant a few feet away.

Natural water basins had formed in the rocks; these were periodically filled with water from the low condensing clouds, as they rose from the plains below. The huge winged birds glided gently down to drink at the watering holes.

Rocks of hundreds of tons lodge sedately on to the tops of small pinnacles, while the greater masses of individual rocks stand as sentinel, guarding their smaller brothers. The wind and rain of the monsoon wreak vengeance and destruction on the sentinels, reducing them slowly year by year, breaking them up and depriving them of their supports until even they go crashing down into the valley below. Alfred thought of the hymn – 'Change and decay, in all around I see'.

As he glanced across the plain below him, Alfred could see a beautiful blue lake. He immediately decided to take the downward course, wending his way over the masses of fallen rocks. The heat of the day made him anxious to shed all his clothes and sink his overheated body into the blue warm waters, oblivious to the possibility of human enemies therein. Refreshed, he made his way back to camp.

Back at Santa Cruz, after the course, Alfred found that part of his squadron, which had been in Ceylon, were returned to Cochin. Their operations were mainly normal convoy escorts and shipping lane patrols, and anti-submarine duties. Above Bombay Harbour, Alfred decided to write and tell his mother of his little exploits of discovery on his off duty walk. He was missing his old friend Sgt Bond. Particularly he remembered the early period when they were in tented accommodation.

Dear Mother,
I have not yet received any mail from you since leaving Egypt. We are near to the jungle here, so very much different to desert life.

Snakes abound, the Indians are busy extending the facilities of the landing grounds. They carry sticks with which to beat the snakes, they seem to think that all snakes are poisonous, I'm certainly not going to fall out with them on that point.

I found myself a stick and set out to climb a big tree covered hill, about four or five miles away. After walking across open land, where Indians were cutting the tall dry undergrowth with scythes, I came upon some fallen coconut trees. One realised the colossal length of them when seeing them lying on the ground. On top of the standing coconut trees perch the huge bald-headed, wicked-looking vultures, with seemingly leering eyes, ever on the alert should you decide to fall dead beneath them.

Eventually I came across huge pipe lines standing some four feet high and crossing the countryside. They were taking water from the hills to supply water to the towns and villages below. As I made to clamber over them, I noticed an Indian boy looking down the side and I saw a yellowish snake with black markings. I went to prod it with my stick, the native boy ran for his life, which made me see sense, so I also beat a quick retreat.

Only a short distance further on, I came to a *wadi*, and something slithered in front of me. It was the biggest snake I'll ever see out of captivity. It was yellowish brown in colour and seemed to be yards and yards in length; to frighten it away I kept beating my stick on the ground as I stepped back a pace.

A little further on amongst the trees, I came upon a big circular well, built of stone and mortar. It must have been an important watering place in days gone by. On the surrounding stonework, at the top of the well, was a marble slab, inscribed on this was: BUILT BY PAUL SANTOS OF SAHAR AD 1829. It measured forty yards round the circumference and the water was only three feet below ground level. I wondered who Paul Santos was of over a century ago. The name sounded romantic; no doubt he was a settler from far off lands – he had left his mark here.

Continuing on my journey over rough country, I eventually came to a river, I slung my shoes and stockings round my neck and started to wade across. There were quite a few eels floating by, on the other side was dense tropical trees of mangrove, and native boys and girls were taking a dip in the water. They came from grass huts hidden inside the darkness of the forest.

A wild-looking man suddenly appeared and stood looking in amazement at this stranger in their midst. I smiled and said '*Saalam*,' the only Hindustani word I knew, for I found myself often using Arabic words. Further along I eventually came to a clearing where there were grass huts with open entrances. The only thing one can see inside is clothing and sleeping equipment.

The natives were very primitive but very industrious. Alfred wondered if India would in the future become a great-World nation again when she took on the mantle of self-government once more.

On the eastern side of the country he thought of all those hundreds of people dying of starvation. Thank goodness Britain was helping out by supplying grain to places like Bengal. This great country had supplied us with wonderful fighting units, serving in different theatres of war.

Now we are here building airports and landing fields which they will take over. I think this will be a futurist country in world affairs. But they have a lot to overcome with races and differing religions. My thoughts must get back to my native path and the interesting visible things around me.

All the trees seem to have stems dropping from the branches down to the ground, making it very dense underneath. I feel like the local fieldmouse in a field of tall grain. The natives are gathering hay and piling it up in the clearing; a few buffalo cows are browsing. A little further on, meadowland with a river running through, water buffalo were wallowing in the mud on the river bank.

Mixed cattle were tied up in a shed, many had calves with their flop ears hanging over their eyes. Britain's contribution to this assortment were a few Alderney and Jersey cows.

Hundreds of rooks were making a terrific din, it was then that I noticed that all the dung from these animals was carted outside, where the natives mould it with their hands into pancakes to lay out to dry on the roofs of the huts. When dry it is used as fuel for cooking.

A small bird of diminutive size is hopping about on a branch of a tree. He has a long tail and has yellowish brown on his breast. There were many beautiful butterflies and the woodpeckers busy searching for tree mites. The rooks were having a happy time riding on the backs of the cows, tick catching. Later I noticed one jumping on the back of a vulture on the top of a coconut tree. The old vulture just turned his head on his long skinny neck and gave the miscreant a look of contempt.

On a eucalyptus tree, I noticed, hanging from a branch, a dome, rather like a bee-hive shape. This had been made by the still-growing green leaves being stuck together by a white substance. I wondered whose home it could be, but soon found out when I touched it with my stick. Immediately thousands of red ants swarmed over the outside and down the stick. These are the kind of ants that can give a good nip, so I beat a quick retreat.

Suddenly I heard the wailing of a terrified child; he appeared round a bend in the path, pursued by a native who was throwing boulders at the little boy. He kept giving a horrible laugh as the boulders came ever nearer to hitting the boy. I shouted to him to stop, and when he caught sight of me he was flabbergasted and suddenly turned tail back to his grass hut. One could not help but wonder at anything happening in the confines of this dark place.

I am now at the top of the hill – my original ambition – what a fine view it is, coconut palms on every side. The sea spreading to the west with ships in the harbour. On the eastern side stretch forests over the hill and dale, but here I am not permitted to give you more details [Bombay Harbour].

A small bird, with a long tail, hovers in the air near a tree flower. It is the honey bird; darting out his long tongue into the centre of the flower to get the honey. A kingfisher flashed by in the speckled sunshine. My few hours of heaven are at an end, I am nearly back at camp.

Your loving son,
Alfred

Most of the teeming millions of humanity of Bombay went about their work, chug, chugging along with charcoal-fired buses, decorated inside and outside, and with Indians of all creeds clinging on the sides and on top. Alfred thought that anything that seemed worn-out to western eyes was just waiting to be brought back to new life by the Indians. The intricate things they could turn out on home-made lathes driven by an upturned tyreless wheel of a cycle, the driving belt riding snugly in the groove of the wheel.

Pedestrians were walking, running, standing, lying down or sitting down; the never ending round of beggars both young and old. The near-dead walking skeleton suddenly sinking down on the road; starvation of body and soul had won its evil battle. The playing of the two-stringed fiddle and other native instruments of music; the rather mournful voice of singers. The red-stained walls, up to three feet from the ground, coloured by the natives spitting out chewed red betel nut.

The *Parsis* – round-minaret-like buildings with shaped spaces to place dead bodies to be cleaned to the bone by vultures, to leave the white bones for disposal, probably into the Ganges River. The *dharma* – teaching of accepting one's conditions and performing the duties appropriate to it. The *karma* – the reward or punishment in the next life. Many of these things were explained to Alfred when he talked with the chief cartoonist of the Bombay paper in the Wayside Inn. It was a new fascinating experience in this great country.

On 14 April 1944, an ammunition ship out at sea caught fire. Great attempts were made to put it out, which was thought to be successful; on instructions from the port authorities they were eventually allowed to sail the ship into Bombay dockyard. No sooner had it entered the busy port, when it blew up with a mighty explosion. No. 203 Squadron personnel were busy on their various duties some miles away, when suddenly a great billowing cloud rose into the air, mushrooming out as it rose. A few moments later came the sound of the violent explosion. The whole ship and everything else around it had gone up in the air. The molten metal from the exploding ammunition spread over the area of the dockyard and adjoining parts of the city. At 19.00 hours, a telephone message was received from the CO ordering the Squadron Fire Service and all available personnel to proceed to the scene of the fire. They were to assist in fire fighting and salvage work; this lasted throughout the night and the next day.

There was, at this time, a serious famine in Madras, the relief of which lay in the form of grain in the warehouses. With a team of men, Alfred was engaged on salvaging the grain from a burning dockside warehouse. Wearing tin hats was essential for burning timbers and falling slates were scattering about them. They were successful in salvaging most of the grain, the rest of it kept popping off with the intense heat. Practically every native had either been killed, or disappeared after the explosion. The whole area was left to the military and police operators. On the street lay an Indian sailor, a piece of water-guttering had gone right through his head, by his temples, and protruded out at either side, giving him the grotesque appearance of some person from outer space.

The sudden impact of the sight set Alfred's mind fleeting over events of the war that he had witnessed. A man sitting calmly in a shot-up lorry with the lower half of his jaw shot away. Men burned to death in tanks. Numerous air crashes that he had been involved with in trying to rescue men from burning planes, and other casualties of war. But Alfred had never imagined an explosion killing a man in this bizarre way.

An English WREN who had been cycling from the docks was blown up and deposited in a tree along with her cycle. The fire was now a raging inferno, covering a wide area of the warehouses; opposite the burning grain store in the adjoining street was a stream of red, blue and green flames which originated from a John Haig's warehouse. The flames came from burning spirits running down the street. Part of the front of the store had been blown away where it exposed stacks of bottles of spirits and cigars. Secretly, the men nearest to it pocketed bottles of spirits before the whole lot exploded into flames. But unbeknown to them, two junior Commonwealth officers had already grabbed several crates of whisky and placed them in their truck.

Lower down the road Corporal Alfred Barker and Corporal Read came upon a lone Indian soldier struggling to direct his hosepipe on to a warehouse full of lorry tyres to try and save them. He was directing the hose onto the tyres themselves, whereas the threat came from the adjoining burning warehouse. Alfred and Corporal Read helped him to turn his hose on to the hot wall of the adjoining warehouse, whilst they then rushed to salvage the tyres.

Other Indian soldiers came to help, in charge of them was a young British lieutenant. He was rushing about in a complete frenzy, pushing and shoving the native troops in all directions, without the slightest idea of organised thought of operation. Corporal Barker and Corporal Read approached the man and told him to get a grip on himself.

From one warehouse to another the airmen worked on salvaging stock, while Corporals Barker and Read again came upon the young British lieutenant. He seemed to be in a bigger frenzy than ever and they could not withstand the sad spectacle any longer. They approached him and told him he was a disgrace to His Majesty's uniform. He threatened to put them on a charge; they told him to get on with his work.

But the sudden collapse of a four-storey building made them all run for safety. After a full night and most of the next day, the grime-covered men made their weary way back to the crossroads by the now burnt-out grain store and John Haig's warehouse.

The two junior Commonwealth officers had already gone back to camp with their booty of two crates of John Haig's whisky. The CO, Wing Commander Masterman, who had been directing operations elsewhere, was unaware of the booty which was to enter his mess surreptitiously. After recuperation at Santa Cruz the following day, word was passed around that the military police were making inquiries about the looting of whisky. Immediately Alfred organised several other NCOs to go round the men's quarters warning them that charges would be brought against them if they had looted property. But all that the NCOs could confiscate were odd bottles of whisky. It was then that a new man to the squadron was going round questioning the men. He was a member of the military police.

Alfred had relieved the men of three full bottles of whisky, and he was desperate to get rid of the evidence. The Indian workmen had just completed building the concrete pillar to a small bridge by the runway. It was still shuttered to hold the wet concrete, and three bottles of John Haig's whisky quickly found a home in the wet concrete.

As he walked away, he thought of that incident in France when they had buried new generator engines in the woods, hoping the Germans would not find them. What fate awaited the whisky bottles?

The military police found no evidence of looting in the airmen's quarters. So they visited the Officer's Mess on the following day; the new duty officer with two crates of whisky unexplained for had booked them in as stock. But with no explanation as to their acquisition.

The result was a court martial to be held in Bombay. Corporal Barker and Corporal Read, being senior in service on the squadron, were called upon to give evidence as to the character of Wing Commander Masterman. They both gave their CO a wonderful reference; they could do no other for he was an exceptionally good commander upholding the good name of his ex-Guardsman position and now RAF *esprit de corps*. He was a breath of fresh air compared to some of their former commanding officers. The two junior officers were both severely reprimanded for they were the real culprits.

A few days later the squadron received confirmation of the good work the squadron had done at the scene of the explosion: 'The Governor of Bombay and Adjutant-General of India thank you in appreciation of the work carried out by 203 Squadron personnel', and from Air Chief Marshal Sir Richard Pierse KCB DSO AFC, Air Commander-in-Chief SEAC.

In June there were reports of suspicious sightings of submarines at Cochin; on their duty 203 Squadron did four anti-submarine searches and twelve convoy escorts in the shipping-lane patrols.

A bomb-aiming competition was also organised, the Commonwealth and Americans taking part. No. 203 Squadron Wellington DJA411 with Captain Flt/Lt Oldsworth and crews and Corporal Alfred acting as flight engineer, flew to Calcutta, El-Marda Road, then on to Thomas Mount, Madras, to take part in the low-level bombing competition.

The next morning, when Alfred was running up the engines of his Wellington, he noticed oil escaping from the propeller feedpipe which ran between the two top cylinders, where the cooling fins of the cylinders had vibrated their way through the feedpipe. Flt/Lt Oldsworth was very upset at the thought of being unable to be a competitor.

Alfred reassured him that by hook or by crook the plane would be ready to take part in the competition, but this was easier said than done. He contacted the technical flight sergeant at the base camp, but was met with, 'I've got no spares for people playing at war, don't you know there's a real war going on.'

'Yes, I do, Sergeant,' said Corporal Barker, 'and do you know if the crews couldn't bomb properly they may as well not be part of it. Could you please lend me a blow lamp then?'

Looking very puzzled at this request of Alfred's, but feeling compassion for his persistence, the flight sergeant went to stores and withdrew a huge blow lamp. He was now intrigued with Alfred, probably he thought Alfred was going to set fire to the hangar.

Several house bricks were placed in a circle to contain the heat from the blow lamp and, after cleaning the fractured oil pipe, Alfred cut a cartridge case to fit over the fracture. He then soldered it into position. The flight sergeant – now a little subdued – said, 'You'd better enter that as a temporary repair in your form 700, Corporal.'

Alfred was now splattered in grime and oil after fitting and testing the temporary repair, but it did the trick. Flight Lieutenant Oldsworth was very pleased that he could take part in the competition and invited Alfred to fly with them. He quickly wiped the oil and sweat off his legs and arms with a petrol-soaked cloth, then nearly went berserk with the pain as the petrol fumes entered his open pores.

Wellington DJA411 and crew from 203 Squadron won the low-level bombing trophy, a huge two-handled silver cup, given by the Maharajah of Mysore.

On returning to Santa Cruz, the Commanding Officer filled the silver cup with punch and the crew all drank from it. Alfred felt proud that once again, against all odds, he had helped to bring 203 Squadron out on top. A short time after this incident DJA411 straddled a submarine with depth charges.

On 21 June an aircraft piloted by F/O Haywood was about to

take off from the short runway at Santa Cruz, when a vehicle was seen to drive on to the runway. The aircraft swung to the left, then to the right, on the runway but ended up in the monsoon-bogged ground, and caught fire. The crew escaped but, as the fire crews could not cross the bog, the plane was burned out. It was understood that a native woman was killed in this accident and her family were paid compensation for the tragedy.

On 18 October the squadron was on the move again, this time to Southern India, to Madurai, but most of the senior NCOs were now posted to other squadrons or sent back to England. On flying down to Madurai during the monsoon period, they were cruising along in the air and Alfred was humming a tune. He had noticed on other occasions, when flying in a Wellington, that you could hum any tune you liked, and somehow or other it would blend in with the tune which was played back to you through the vibrations of the geodetic construction of the plane. On this occasion he was standing up, looking through the astra-dome of the plane, admiring the vista of a huge stepped hill. Above each step the natives had woven an intricate pattern of agriculture, but now the heavy rains pouring down on to this vast network were wreaking havoc. It was washing away the soil, taking it on to each lower step in turn, until the brown muddy sludge found its way into the river below, transforming this into a moving mass of brown soup. Suddenly he noticed an oil substance speckling its sticky spots on to the astradome. His first thoughts were, My God – the engines, but then as more rational thoughts took hold, he realised it was hydraulic oil.

Immediately he went down the fuselage to look at the hydraulic oil indicator above the navigator's head. He saw that it was below the red danger line. Not wanting to upset the crew, he whispered to the pilot that they had an hydraulic leak and they must land fairly quickly. The pilot informed the navigator to peruse his charts for the possibility of finding a landing strip. After a few minutes the navigator said, 'Thank God for that, there's a new landing strip being constructed hereabouts, let us circle round.' As they took a large circular movement they noticed a brilliant white runway below them, part of which ended up towards the jungle. The navigator explained, 'Perhaps the concrete's not set yet.' Cheerful bloke, the navigator, thought Alfred.

Fingers were crossed as the pilot operated the undercarriage and flaps mechanism. A considerable amount of fuel was in the tanks, a crash now could send them all up in smoke. Fortunately both flaps and undercarriage worked, they touched ground and the concrete held the weight of the plane. They brought the plane to a standstill at the far end of the new runway where Indian natives were still working on clearing trees and undergrowth. Half-clad natives with machetes and knives in their hands appeared from the cover of the mango trees, offering the crew freshly picked mangoes.

In the meantime, Alfred investigated the problem of the oil leak and found that the screw cap of the hydraulic tank had not been tightened down sufficiently, in consequence of which the slipstream from the propellers had been entering the threaded portion into the tank. It had siphoned off the oil through the breather hole of the cap. The natives were now prodding and pulling at the plane, for it was the nearest they had ever been to one. Alfred shouted to the pilot to start up the engines otherwise they would have no plane to fly. As the engines roared into life, the natives ran for their lives into the cover of the jungle. The crew continued on their way to Madurai where their planes were soon operating around Ceylon (now Sri Lanka) and the Gulf of Mannar.

On 17 November 1944 word came through to Alfred of one of the greatest explosions of the war, apart from nuclear bombs. The great underground storage of thousands of tons of explosives at Fauld, near Burton-on-Trent, went up in a mighty explosion killing over seventy people. A man was working on the land, with a tractor – neither he nor his tractor was ever seen again. The explosion was blamed on members of the Armaments Inspectorate, for RAF and civilians being allowed to work with tools that could cause an explosion. Even prisoners of war were working there, for five Italian prisoners were killed.

The last senior NCO was now posted from Alfred's unit, so he was now acting flight sergeant and his term of service was coming to an end. The technical officer approached him and asked him if he would consider staying with the squadron if he was offered promotion. He was now suffering from conjunctivitis, so he decided to return to England at the end of his overseas commitments. Having served with the same squadron in Aden on the Abyssinian Campaign and nearly three years of Western Desert warfare, and then in India, preparing for self-rule, he felt he had had enough.

The welfare committee, on hearing of Corporal (Colonel) Barker's intended departure, presented him with a cigarette case, the inside of which had been inscribed with 'Cpl. "Colonel" Barker', in recognition of his welfare work on 203 Squadron in Egypt and the Far East. Apparently the overriding need to relieve boredom in the far-off lonely places of wartime service was well understood by the men, but not always by some of their commanding officers.

On 13 November, Alfred and thousands of other troops were herded together to meet up at their secret port of departure. The ship that was earmarked for returning them to England had been hit by a U-boat and her side had been ripped open. After several weeks of inactivity and utter boredom, they were loaded on to a ship which had just delivered new troops for the Far East conflict, including WAAFS. Her decks were dirty, and discarded condoms were in evidence below decks. Alfred reflected that in all his wartime service he had always served with male troops. The men were herded below decks and placed in three layers, one lot lying on the floor on blankets, one layer on the tables and the other layer swinging above in hammocks. The only outlet for them was that one gangway. The only lighting was red spot lamps leading up the gangway to the upper decks.

Alfred remarked to his NCO neighbour, 'If we're hit by a torpedo, this deck will be a death trap.' Suddenly, after rounding the point of India, all the ship's alarm systems were belting out their deadly warning of submarine attack. Immediately pandemonium was let loose, men jumping out of hammocks and dropping on to men on tables and then on to those poor souls on the floor. All in a mad endeavour to gain access to the dimly lit gangway and the upper decks, and all with but one desire, and that was self-preservation. The entrance to the gangway was a mass of struggling bodies, some were being trampled on. Alfred's mind always seemed to race ahead of his thoughts on such occasions. He started to bellow out, 'Steady lads, it's only a dummy run, they're only testing us. Keep a bit of order.' His fellow NCO took up the same steadying cry. The men were reassured and eventually all found their way on the upper deck to be immediately ordered to don lifejackets. Eventually the danger of being torpedoed passed and they all breathed freely again. Alfred reflected that the brave Navy men were constantly facing these hazardous situations.

On 13 January, they eventually landed at Liverpool. It was 13 February 1945 when Alfred obtained leave and his recorded overseas service ended on 13 January 1945. He was then posted to Bottesford, 1668 Con Unit, and on to 91 Group Cottesmore.

On 6 August 1945 the atom bomb was exploded and Alfred thought it a decisive factor towards the ending of the war. He was now working with a depleted team of men on changing engines on Lancasters; when they were declared serviceable they were flown away to be discarded as scrap. The authorities were a little uneasy at this particular time with quite a large number of people very pro-Russian; times were tricky. After early pre-war service on the old bi-planes, and making do with second-rate planes in the early stages of the war, Alfred felt sad to see those wonderful planes take off from the drome, never to be seen again.

Alfred was on the reserve list until 29 April 1946.

9

A New Life Begins

AFTER so many devoted years of service to his country in wartime, Alfred now faced the prospect of an uncertain future in civilian life. There were now thousands of demobilised ex-servicemen seeking housing and jobs.

The flying-training school at Burnaston in Derbyshire was about to be turned over to a civilian airline to be called Derby Airways. Alfred obtained a position there as a fitter and was engaged on the major overhaul of their first airliner, a Dragon-Rapide, purchased from the Royal Air Force.

The working arrangements in the hangar, for the testing of carburettors, was rather a makeshift affair. A five-gallon drum of petrol was pumped up to pressure by a foot pump. It was then fed to the carburettor by pipeline for testing. An oil-fired decarbonising outfit stood opposite on the floor of the hangar. A leak occurred in the pipeline, a sheet of petrol-vapour was sent across the corner of the hangar to where the oil-fired stove stood.

Alfred was quick to see the danger: 'Put out that stove,' but it was too late, there was a blinding flash in front of the men's faces. They had no alternative but to rush through the flames. Alfred's demobilisation suit was burned to a cinder.

The company later moved to Castle Donnington Airport and was now known as the British Midland Airways. Burnaston was later to become the Toyota factory.

In the early days of British Midland Airways there was very little provision made for the accommodation of aircrews. An ancient Inn – called The George – came up for sale near the airport. The sale was conducted by the auctioneer in the village square. In his address he advised that part of it was only fit for demolishing.

Alfred turned to his wife, who stood by his side. 'It would break my heart to see this old place demolished, my father brought me here by pony and trap when I was a little boy. In those days the second greatest horse fair of England was held here.'

Alfred's wife gave his arm a friendly squeeze, 'We'll see what it gets up to in price, Alfred.' And for two thousand five hundred pounds they became the proud but anxious owners of a derelict inn.

With hard work and dedication, and with the aid of a local builder, they transformed the George Inn into a guest house. Alfred approached the director of British Midland Airways to make an agreement to provide accommodation for his aircrew.

When converting the inn they discovered an old bricked-in fireplace and a woman's lace-up shoe. It was full of what they thought were gold sovereigns, but they later turned out to be brass gaming counters. They were specially made for the Princess Charlotte Inn in Oxford Street, London.

This find in such an ancient place, in later years set the adrenaline flowing to buy Bentley Hall at Hungary Bentley. It stood by the side of the Roman road leading to the Roman camp of Rocester. Dry-moated, it was mentioned in the Domesday book.

The property was originally owned by the Ferrers and Blount families, and later by a Thomas Browne, who married the second daughter, Dorothy Vernon, of Sudbury Hall. The East Wing, with its attractive pillared portico supporting a bold bay window, was Jacobean but inside the half-timbered walls and slightly sloping floors suggested an earlier Tudor or Elizabethan period. A large central chimney had been bricked up. Alfred was keen to uncover the secrets within and discovered the huge domed fireplaces of earlier times. There was a dog-legged staircase leading up to the upper storeys and the servants' attic quarters.

The West Wing jutted out from the East Wing in its entirely

different style. It was believed that this wing, of early Queen Anne with segmented pediment and Corinthian pilasters, was designed by the Sudbury Hall architect, Sir William Wilson.

When restoring the Hall, part of the West Wing had to be taken down and each part numbered and stored, ready for replacement under the watchful eye of the historical architect.

The village of Hungary Bentley has long since disappeared but the house foundations lie in the nearby fields. It is believed that a passage was built in the sixteenth and seventeenth centuries to the former priory of Stydd Hall, Yeaveley, and, in 1586, Edward Bentley of Bentley Hall was found guilty of high treason and was hanged when Mary Queen of Scots was kept at nearby Tutbury Castle. Was he involved in the plot to remove her from Tutbury to hide her at Bentley Hall...?

Dedication window at Rolls-Royce

Postscript

WHILE writing the last page of this manuscript the beautiful sound of a flying Spitfire was heard overhead. It was RM689, giving a display over Rolls-Royce.

The ground crew at Hucknall had looked after RM689 for thirty years and colleagues in East Kilbride did so much to provide the Griffon engine and to keep it going so superbly, and those at Bristol, Hucknall and Derby ensured that she would be capable of flying so well into the next century. She did so much to uphold the great name of Rolls-Royce. But tragedy struck at Woodford, when she was lost with her pilot Dave Moore, who will be sadly missed.

Mr M. J. Bradbury, who lived near the East Midlands Airport, wrote the following poem, a fitting tribute to this wonderful little loveable monoplane.

The Griffon engines Rolls-Royce Spitfire lost for ever
at the Woodford Airshow 1992

I will miss the Rolls-Royce Spitfire,
And the magic sound it made,
With its powerful Griffon engine,
So exciting when displayed.
I've watched and listened so many times
From the Midlands down to Kent,

Always thrilled by the sight and sound
And knowing what it meant.

Fliers so long ago now,
Fighting for our lives,
Many giving their own away,
So that we might survive,
Flying Hurricanes and Spitfires
And other fighters too
Many with Merlin engines
But Griffons in a few.

Although our Rolls-Royce Spitfire
Never saw much war,
She was a superb reminder
Of all Spits built before.
Based at Donnington Airport
That was her home base
From where I live I gaze south-west
With sadness on my face.

Appendix

No. 203 Squadron

Badge:
A winged sea horse

Motto:
Occidens oriensque
(West and East)

No. 203 Squadron was formed on 1 April 1918 at Treizennes in northern France from No. 3 Squadron RNAS on its absorption into the newly-formed Royal Air Force. Equipped with Camels, it flew fighter and ground attack missions over the Western Front for the rest of the war. Reduced to a cadre in March 1919, it returned to the UK and disbanded on 21 January 1920. On 1 March 1920, No. 203 was reformed at Leuchars as a fleet fighter squadron. It flew Camels and Nightjars and in the last three months of 1922 was sent to Turkey during the Chanak crisis. The squadron was redesignated No. 402 Flight on 1 April 1923.

On 1 January 1929, No. 482 (Coastal Reconnaissance) Flight at Mount Batten was redesignated No. 203 Squadron and in February it left the UK with three Southampton flying boats, arriving at its new base in Iraq in mid-March. Patrols over the Persian Gulf were taken over by Rangoons in 1931 which were in turn replaced by Singapores in 1935. In September 1935, these were taken to Aden during the Abyssinian crisis and returned to Iraq in August 1936. The squadron returned to Aden on the outbreak of World War Two but began to convert to Blenheims in December 1939, receiving its own aircraft in March 1940. When Italy entered the war in June 1940, No. 203's Blenheims flew reconnaissance and fighter patrols over the Red Sea until April 1941, when the squadron moved to Egypt and Palestine. After taking part in the Syrian campaign, it began reconnaissance missions over the Eastern Mediterranean and received some Marylands in February 1942. Baltimores were added in August 1942 and in November the squadron was fully equipped with the type. In November 1943, No. 203 moved to India where it converted to Wellingtons for coastal patrol duties. These were replaced by Liberators in October 1944 and anti-shipping patrols began from Ceylon in February 1945, continuing for the rest of the war. After a period of transport duties in South-East Asia, No. 203 returned to the UK in May 1946 and converted to Lancasters. These were flown until the arrival of Neptunes in March 1953 which were in service until the squadron disbanded on 1 September 1956. On 1 November 1958, No. 240 Squadron at Ballykelly was renumbered 203 Squadron and flew Shackletons on maritime patrols duties from Northern Ireland until the beginning of 1969, when the squadron moved to Malta. Early in 1972, having convened to Nimrods, difficulties arose over the use of Maltese bases and No. 203 was transferred to the NATO base at Signonella in Sicily, returning in April to Luqa. The squadron was disbanded on 31 December 1977.

Squadron bases

Treizennes	1 Apr 1918	Kabrit	16 Apr 1941
Lièttres	9 Apr 1918	Heraklion	24 Apr 1941
Filescamp	16 May 1918	Kabrit	30 Apr 1941
Allonville	14 Aug 1918	LG.101	20 Jun 1941
Filescamp	6 Sep 1918	Berka 3	16 Jan 1942
Izel-le-Hameau	23 Sep 1918	El Gubbi	24 Jan 1942
Bruille	24 Oct 1918	Gambut	1 Feb 1942
Auberchicourt	24 Nov 1918	LG.05	3 Feb 1942
Orcq	22 Dec 1918	LG.39	6 Feb 1942
Boisdinghem	18 Jan 1919	LG.Y	30 Jun 1942
Waddington	27 Mar 1919	LG.X	9 Jul 1942
?copwick	Dec 1919	LG.227	17 Oct 1942
	to 21 Jan 1920	Berka 3	4 Mar 1943
Leuchars	1 Mar 1920	LG.91	4 Nov 1943
HMS Argus	18 Sep 1922	Santa Cruz	15 Nov 1943
Kilya Bay	27 Sep 1922	Madura	9 Oct 1944
HMS Argus	19 Dec 1922	Kankesanturai	19 Feb 1945
Leuchars	4 Jan 1923	Leuchars	22 May 1946
	to 1 Apr 1923	St Eval	16 Jan 1947
Mount Batten	1 Jan 1929	St Mawgan	16 Apr 1952
Left for Iraq	28 Feb 1929	St Eval	26 May 1952
Basra	14 Mar 1929	Topcliffe	12 Aug 1952
Aden	26 Sep 1935		to 1 Sep 1956
Basra	24 Aug 1936	Ballykelly	1 Nov 1958
Aden/Isthmus	2 Sep 1939	Luqa	1 Feb 1969
Sheikh Othman	15 Feb 1940	Sigonella	12 Jan 1972
Khormaksar	18 May 1940	Luqa	23 Apr 1972
			to 31 Dec 1977

Aircraft Equipment	Period of service	Representative Serial	
Camel	Apr 1918 – Mar 1919	N6461	
	Mar 1920 – Aug 1922		
Nightjar	Aug 1922 – Apr 1923	J6938	
Southampton II	Jan 1929 – Apr 1931	S1300	(C)
Fairey IIIF	Mar 1929 – Apr 1929	J9060	
Rangoon	Feb 1931 – Nov 1935	S1433	
Singapore III	Sep 1935 – Mar 1940	K4584	(PP–C)
Blenheim I	Mar 1940 – May 1940	L8545	
Blenheim IV	May 1940 – Nov 1942	T1988	(V)
Maryland I	Feb 1942 – Nov 1942	AH280	(Y)
Hudson II, III	Feb 1942 – Mar 1942	T9397	
Baltimore I, II, IIIA, V	Aug 1942 – Nov 1943	FA107	(F)
Wellington XIII	Nov 1943 – Oct 1944	JA411	(D)
Liberator VI	Oct 1944 – Mar 1946	KG911	(D)
Liberator GR8	Jan 1946 – Oct 1946	KL565	(CJ–B)
Lancaster GR3	Aug 1946 – Mar 1953	RF311	(CJ–G)
Neptune MR1	Mar 1953 – Sep 1956	WX518	(B–J)
Shackleton MRI	Nov 1958 – Sep 1959	WB860	
Shackleton MR2	Jul 1962 – Dec 1966	WL742	(H)
Shackleton MR3	Dec 1958 – Jul 1962	WR974	(F)
	Jun 1966 – Jan 1972	XF708	(C)
Nimrod MR1	Jul 1971 – Dec 1977	XV257	(57)